T0135208

Graphical Simulation of Deformable Models

Jianping Cai · Feng Lin · Hock Soon Seah

Graphical Simulation
of Deformable Models

 Springer

Jianping Cai
Nanyang Technological University
Singapore
Singapore

Hock Soon Seah
Nanyang Technological University
Singapore
Singapore

Feng Lin
School of Computer Engineering
Nanyang Technological University
Singapore
Singapore

ISBN 978-3-319-84549-4   ISBN 978-3-319-51031-6   (eBook)
DOI 10.1007/978-3-319-51031-6

Printed on acid-free paper

This Springer imprint is published by Springer Nature
The registered company is Springer International Publishing AG
The registered company address is: Gewerbestrasse 11, 6330 Cham, Switzerland

Preface

This book is on dynamics simulation of deformable objects. We are especially interested in the simulation of deformable models with anisotropic materials, which is less exploited in existing research. To do this, it is essential to improve the physical realism of simulation, since many real-world objects have complex mechanical rather than isotropic properties. An in-depth survey is conducted on the relevant research topics. Both physically-based and geometrically-based approaches are studied, and our contributions are made in modeling and controlling of anisotropic dynamics deformations.

To prepare the ground for dynamics simulation with the finite element method, we first introduce a previously developed mesh representation algorithm, *isosurface stuffing*, which fills an object domain with a uniformly sized tetrahedral mesh. This algorithm is numerically robust. It generates tetrahedra from a small set of pre-computed stencils. A variant of the algorithm creates a mesh with internal grading. That is, on the boundary where high resolution is desired, the tetrahedral elements are fine and uniformly sized; and in the interior, the tetrahedra may be coarser and vary in size. This combination of features makes isosurface stuffing a suitable tool for large-deformation mechanics.

We then investigate transversely isotropic materials for the simulation of deformable objects with fibrous structures. In previous work, direction-dependent behaviors of transversely isotropic materials can only be achieved with an additional energy function which incorporates the material preferred direction. Such an additional energy term increases the computational complexity. We introduce a *fiber-field incorporated corotational finite element model* (CLFEM) that works directly with a constitutive model of transversely isotropic material. A smooth *fiber-field* is used to establish the local frames for each element. The orientation information of each element is incorporated into the CLFEM model by adding local transformations onto each element of the stiffness matrix.

We further introduce deformation simulation for orthotropic materials. An orthotropic deformation controlling *frame-field* is conceptualized and a frame construction tool is developed for users to define the desired material properties. A quaternion Laplacian smoothing algorithm is designed for propagating the user-defined sparsely distributed frames into the entire object. The orthotropic frame-field is coupled with the CLFEM model to complete an orthotropic deformable model.

And finally, we present an integrated real-time system for animation of skeletal characters with anisotropic tissues. Existing geometrically-based skinning techniques suffer from obvious volume distortion artifact, and they cannot produce secondary dynamic motions, such as *jiggling* effects. *Physically-based skinning* with FEM models has high computational cost that restricts its practical applications. To solve these problems, we introduce a strain-based *Position based Dynamics* (PBD) framework for skeletal animation. It bridges the gap between geometric models and physically-based models, and achieves both efficient and physically-plausible performance. Natural secondary motion of soft tissues is produced. Anisotropic deformations are made possible with separately defined stretch and shear properties of the material, using the user-designed *frame-field*. Owing to the efficiency and stability of our proposed layered constraint solving scheme, we can achieve real-time performance, and the system is robust with large deformations and degenerate cases.

The monograph is written for researchers who would like to develop their own algorithms. The important mathematical and computational concepts are presented together with illustrations and working examples. It can also be used as a reference book for graduate students and senior undergraduates in the area of computer graphics, computer animation, and virtual reality. Academics, researchers, etc. will find this to be an exceptional resource.

Enjoy the read.

Singapore
October 2016

Jianping Cai
Feng Lin
Hock Soon Seah

Acknowledgements

We are thankful to our colleagues, Dr. Qian Kemao, Dr. Lee Yong Tsui and Dr. Wu Zhongke. We have benefited a lot from their inspirational suggestions and helpful discussions during the development of this book.

We are also thankful to Dr. Movania Muhammad Mobeen, Dr. Wei Ming Chiew, Dr. Xu Xiang, Liu Hui, Kuleesha Yadav, and Hao Shuji for their discussions in the research.

Contents

Notational Conventions

Most symbols in this work are denoted according to the notational conventions as follows:

Notations

Scalar: a (*Italic* lowercase)
Vector: $\boldsymbol{a}$ (*Italic* and bold lowercase)
Matrix and Tensor: A (Italic and uppercase)
Space of n dimensional real numbers: $\mathbb{R}^n$
Space of $m \times n$ real matrices: $\mathbb{R}^{m \times n}$
Identity matrix: I

Operations

Dot product: "·"such as $\boldsymbol{a} \cdot \boldsymbol{b}$;
Cross product of vector: "×", such as $\boldsymbol{a} \times \boldsymbol{b}$;
Tensor product of two vectors: "⊗", such as $\boldsymbol{a} \otimes \boldsymbol{b}$
Double product or double contraction of two matrices: ":", such as $A{:}B$

List of Figures

List of Tables

Chapter 1
Introduction

Abstract In this chapter, we introduce the objectives of dynamics simulation of deformable objects. We conduct an in-depth survey on the relevant research topics, especially the simulation of deformable models with anisotropic materials, which is less exploited in existing research. We are motivated to improve the physical realism of simulation, since many real-world objects have complex mechanical rather than isotropic properties. Both physically-based and geometrically-based approaches are studied, and our contributions are made in modeling and control of anisotropic dynamics deformations.

Deformable models have been studied for nearly three decades in computer graphics since the late 1980s. In this chapter, we introduce some influential works that have fueled the development of modeling and simulation of deformable objects in the graphics community. Our research focus is on *efficiency*, *stability*, *controllability* and *accuracy* of dynamics simulation.

First, we introduce the **geometrically-based deformable models**, which formulate a mathematical model of deformable objects from a geometric perspective rather than rigorous physics. Some deformation approaches in *geometry processing* are introduced. A group of *position-based methods* for dynamics simulation are discussed. Although being geometrically motivated, these models are related to physical models to some extent, with constraints based on physical principles.

Secondly, we briefly review a simple physical model of **mass spring system** and its extension to particle systems.

Thirdly, we give a comprehensive introduction to the **physically-based deformable models** based on continuum mechanics, from which we initiated our research. Continuum-based models in combination with finite element discretization can produce physically-realistic results. However, in graphics applications, they encounter challenges related to high computational complexity, numerical instability and controllability. Various approaches have been proposed to solve these problems, and we analyze them from different perspectives.

© Springer International Publishing Switzerland 2016
J. Cai et al., *Graphical Simulation of Deformable Models*,
DOI 10.1007/978-3-319-51031-6_1

Fourthly, we introduce some ***hybrid models*** developed in recent years, which attempt to reconcile geometrical methods with physical models and bridge the gap between these two groups, leading to new research potentials.

And finally, we broadly introduce the ***deformation control*** methods, which provide users with control over material properties or complex deformation behaviors.

1.1 Geometrically-Based Methods

See Fig. 1.1.

1.1.1 Deformable Models in Shape Editing

Elastic models are commonly used in *geometry processing*, such as *morphing*, *shape space interpolation*, and *shape editing*. Note that here 'elastic models' refer to *elasticity-inspired* models, which utilize geometric quantities to define elasticity but not according to rigorous physics (i.e., continuum mechanics). Here we only refer to some deformation methods in *shape editing* (i.e., *handle-based shape deformations*) that are related to our research. Other methods such as *free form deformation* are not discussed here, and readers can refer to [1–3] for more details.

In some shape modeling process, users set some vertices of a mesh fixed in position (as *anchor points*) and select a region-of-interest (ROI) for manipulation (as *handles*). The orientation and position of the ROI are interactively manipulated, and then transformations (such as translations and rotations) of the ROI are propagated smoothly to the rest of the shape by deforming the unconstrained part. A basic requirement is that local details of the shape should be preserved during deformations. As shown in Fig. 1.2, the green region represents the handle for manipulation, and the red region is fixed in position as anchor points.

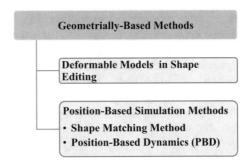

Fig. 1.1 Geometrically-based deformable models

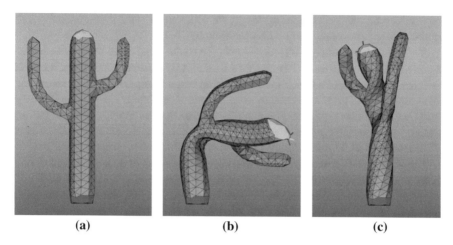

Fig. 1.2 As-rigid-as-possible surface editing. **a** The initial shape; **b** bending deformation; **c** twisting deformation

Figure 1.2a shows the original shape, and Fig. 1.2b, c show the bending and twisting deformations respectively.

A brief review of a prominent work by Sorkine et al. [4], called *as-rigid-as-possible* (ARAP) surface deformation, is described here: given a triangle mesh S consisting of n vertices, it is decomposed into overlapping cells (e.g., the one-ring-neighboring triangles $N(i)$ of each vertex i). The key idea is that the transformation of each cell should be kept as-rigid-as-possible. For a cell C_i corresponding to a vertex i and its deformed counterpart C_i' in the deformed mesh S', a deformation energy (called *local rigidity* energy) is defined by summing up the *deviations from rigidity* of all the cells:

$$E(S') = \sum_{i=1}^{n} \omega_i \sum_{j \in N(i)} \omega_{ij} \left\| \left(\boldsymbol{p}_i' - \boldsymbol{p}_j' \right) - R_i(\boldsymbol{p}_i - \boldsymbol{p}_j) \right\|^2, \quad (1.1)$$

where $\boldsymbol{p}_i$ and $\boldsymbol{p}_i'$ are the vertex positions, and ω_i and ω_{ij} are per-cell and per-edge weights respectively. The matrix $R_i = R_i(S') \in \mathbb{R}^{3 \times 3}$ is the rotation of a cell from S to S', which depends on the deformed shape S'. In order to preserve local details, this nonlinear *rigidity energy* needs to be minimized. Sorkine et al. proposed an *alternating optimization strategy*, which is an iterative process consisting of a local solver and a global solver: in the local step, the rotation R_i of each cell is computed by a *singular value decomposition* of a covariance matrix; in the global step, a global deformation state is obtained by solving a convex quadratic minimization problem.

This alternating approach decomposes a nonlinear minimization problem into two simple sub-problems, which guarantees convergence. Another advantage is its computational efficiency, due to the facts that: (1) the local solving step can be done in parallel (i.e., parallel computing for all the cells), and (2) the system matrix of the global solver is constant and can be pre-factored.

A similar idea of energy formulation can be found in an early work in Laplacian surface editing [5]. Both of the methods formulate a *deformation energy* based on changes of local details, which is essentially in terms of *differential representations* (here, *Laplacian coordinates* are used to encode local details). This idea is further investigated in many works. For example, a skeleton augmented ARAP method was presented in [6] for better volume preservation of a surface mesh; Zhou et al. [7] extended it to volumetric mesh editing using *volumetric graph Laplacian*.

The idea of using an *alternating local/global scheme* to solve a complex non-linear optimization problem is very attractive, due to its efficiency and stability. It was further exploited in physically-based models such as the fast mass-spring system in [8] and the projective dynamics approach in [9].

The idea of finding a *linear transformation* between an original shape and a deformed counterpart inspired the development of *shape matching method* [10]. The corotational FEM model [11, 12] also shares a similar spirit in terms of finding local rotational transformations.

This kind of geometrically-based deformation models (*Laplacian deformation methods*) was further analyzed by Chao et al. [13], which provided a connection between these *physics-like* geometrical models and physical models in solid mechanics.

Our work is related to the Laplacian deformation method [5], not from the perspective of the formulation of elastic deformation energy, but from the way of propagating transformations smoothly.

1.1.2   Position-Based Simulation Methods

Formulations of classical continuum-based dynamics simulation are *force-based*, where internal forces caused by deformation are computed and positions are evolved through numerical integration of accelerations and velocities. In contrast, position-based simulation methods are purely geometrically motivated. By replacing deformation energies with geometric constraints, they modify positions directly and omit the velocity and acceleration layer.

We firstly introduce *shape matching methods*, and then move to *position-based dynamics* (PBD) that becomes popular recently in real-time applications.

1.1.2.1   Shape Matching Method

The shape matching method proposed by Müller et al. [10] is a geometrically-motivated approach [14]. Its key idea is intuitive and simple as shown in Fig. 1.3: given two sets of particles with x_i^0 as an initial configuration and

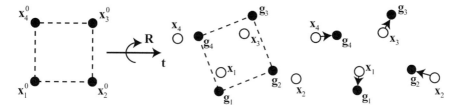

Fig. 1.3 Shape matching method [10]. *Left* is the initial configuration x_i^0; *Middle* is a deformed configuration x_i, and g_i is the computed *goal* positions; *Right* during deformation, x_i is pulled towards its corresponding g_i

x_i as a deformed configuration with mass m_i, a *goal position* g_i is firstly obtained by a rigid transformation (a rotation R and a translation t) that transforms x_i^0 to x_i. The particles of the deformed set x_i are pulled towards the goal positions in order to restore its original shape at each time step. Therefore, this method does not require particle connection information, i.e., it is a meshless method.

An extended *Lattice Shape Matching* (LSM) [15] method uses a regular lattices discretization of a deformable object in order to support large deformations. *Adaptive lattices* are considered in [16], which can support dynamic adaptive selection of level of details and handle topological change. The shape matching method is also employed in a real-time *example-based* dynamics simulation [17].

Müller et al. [18] later extended the shape matching method to *oriented particles* (as shown in Fig. 1.4). By adding *orientation* information, it solves the ill-conditioned matching problem caused by co-linear or co-planar particles.

The shape matching can be seen as a type of constraint projection, which can be directly integrated into the *position-based dynamics* framework discussed below.

1.1.2.2 Position-Based Dynamics

In recent years, position-based dynamics (PBD) becomes popular for simulation of deformable objects (refer to the survey paper [19]), and has been implemented in many high-end products, such as *PhysX, Havok Cloth, Maya nCloth*, and *Bullet Physics Engine* [20].

A classical PBD framework [21] performs a simulation loop in three steps:

(1) The next-time-step positions are first predicted by a simple symplectic integration, which takes into account only external forces. Thus there is no need for computation of internal forces and stiffness matrix as in continuum-based models;

(2) Then, the *predicted positions* are corrected with respect to some geometric constraints, such as area constraints, bending constraints [22] and volume constraints [23], which are solved by a Gauss-Seidel-type method. This procedure is called *position projection* (or, *constraint projection*).

(3) Finally, the velocities are updated, which might also be damped.

Fig. 1.4 Oriented particles
representation [18]

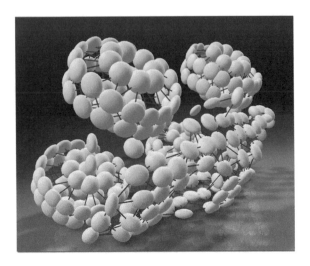

1.1.2.3 Exploiting the PDB Framework

Though a simple explicit time integration scheme is used, the PBD method can avoid *overshooting problem*, because the predicted positions are always projected towards well-defined shapes. They can easily handle collision constraints. Due to their simplicity, efficiency and stability, they are particularly useful in interactive environments such as computer games, where only *visual plausibility* is required.

One problem with these methods is that material behaviors not only depend on constraint parameters, but also depend on the time-step size and the number of iterations in the constraint solver. The Gauss-Seidel-type solver converges faster than the Jacobi-type solver (e.g., [8]), but it can hardly be used for parallel computing. We refer the reader to the papers [19, 24, 25] for more details on the PBD method.

In our work, we have exploited the PBD framework to develop a skeletal animation system, which achieves real-time and stable performance. Continuum-based constraint is used in our system, instead of geometric constraints used here.

1.2 Mass Spring System and Particles System

Among physically-based deformable models, a *mass-spring model* is a rather simple model that was commonly used in the past [8, 26–30]. As a non-rigorous physical model, it represents a deformable object by a spring-network of mass points. Each massless spring (an edge of a discretized mesh) connects two points with masses m_i, m_j, positions x_i, x_j and velocities v_i, v_j respectively, as shown in Fig. 1.5.

Fig. 1.5 A mass spring
connecting two points

The internal force along a spring is computed using the *Hooke's Law*, such that

$$f = \frac{x_j - x_i}{\left|x_j - x_i\right|} \left(k_s \left(\left|x_j - x_i\right| - L_i\right) + k_d \left|v_j - v_i\right|\right),$$

where k_s is the stretch stiffness, k_d the damping coefficient, and L_i is its rest length.

The mass-spring concept can be further generalized to a *particles system* that has the same mesh representation. However, the internal forces are computed differently, which is derived as the gradient of a deformation energy defined in terms of some constraints. Given a constraint function $C(p_1, \ldots, p_n) = 0$, the deformation energy is defined as $U = \frac{1}{2} k \cdot C^2$, with k as the stiffness of the constraint, which is equal to zero at the initial pose. The internal forces are then computed as $f = \frac{\partial U}{\partial p}$. Therefore, more general types of springs can be defined, such as distant-spring, angular-spring, area-spring, and volume-spring [31, 32].

A state-of-the-art work on the mass-spring system was recently proposed by Liu et al. [8]. It reformulates the implicit Euler integration of equations of motion as an energy minimization problem, and achieves much faster and stable performance than the former mass-spring methods.

Modeling of a mass-spring system is straightforward. Due to its low computational complexity, real-time performance can be obtained. However, it has the following drawbacks that limit its applications:

- It is not based on strict physics laws; thus it can hardly obtain physically accurate results;
- It is difficult for users to tune the spring constants for a specific material, which means it is hard to control the mechanical behaviors;
- Deformations depend on mesh discretization, which means that the mechanical behaviors depend on the topology of the spring-mesh.

1.3   Physically-Based Deformable Models

Physically-based deformable models actually originate from continuum mechanics [33, 34]. The continuum-based problem is commonly discretized and solved numerically by the *finite element method* (FEM) [35, 36]. Since the pioneering work by Terzopoulos et al. [37] on elastic models, physically based deformable models have been an active research area in computer graphics (Fig. 1.6).

For most graphics applications such as animations, computer games, visual effects and virtual reality, physics simulation only plays a small part in the whole

Fig. 1.6 Physically-based
deformable models

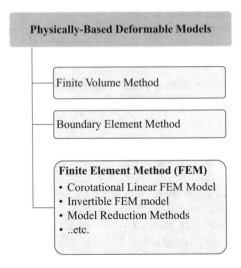

Fig. 1.6 Physically-based
deformable models

system. In contrast to physical models in *mechanical engineering* that require high
accuracy, researchers in computer graphics [24, 38–40] have made more efforts to
achieve the goals of better stability, faster performance, and more controls over
mechanical behaviors. There are always trade-offs between these goals and physical
accuracy. Different models with specific concerns have been proposed, which are
discussed below.

1.3.1 Stability-Concerned Models

Stability of simulation is of great concern for many applications. For example, if a
simulation failed due to numerical instability in a game, it is not possible to re-run it
(i.e., there is no second chance to correct it). Therefore, stability is more important
than accuracy in this kind of scenarios.

Numerical instability is commonly caused by large deformations, large stiffness
of system, large time steps, etc. In this section, we discuss some approaches dealing
with these issues.

1.3.1.1 Large Deformations with Linear Models

Large deformations are quite common in graphics applications. A linear FEM
model is computationally much more efficient than nonlinear FEM models; however, it is not rotation invariant, meaning that obvious volume distortions occur
when a linear model is under large deformations. As shown in Fig. 1.7b, the
volume of the simulated object gets inflated due to a large external force.

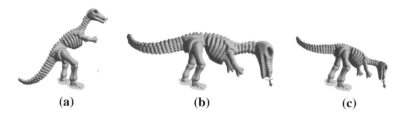

(a)   (b)   (c)

Fig. 1.7 Comparison of linear FEM and CLFEM. **a** is the original shape; **b** shows the inflated-volume artifact with linear FEM; **c** shows the corrected deformation with CLFEM FEM. *Red arrow* represents the external load

To solve this problem, Müller et al. [11, 12] proposed a *corotational FEM model* (CLFEM, also called *warped stiffness model*). The CLFEM model removes the factor of rigid rotational transformation in the computation of internal forces, which makes it rotation invariant. As shown in Fig. 1.7c, the CLFEM model allows large deformations and maintains well-preserved volume. Essentially being a linear elastic model, the CLFEM model can achieve deformation results comparable to a nonlinear FEM model, but at a much less computational cost.

Here, rotation matrices between the initial and deformed shapes are obtained by *polar decomposition*. A less costly approximation was implemented by Allard et al. [41]. Georgii et al. [42] proposed an energy minimization method to get a more stable corotational formulation, and used a multi-grid FEM solver to further improve simulation performance.

1.3.1.2 Degenerate and Inverted Elements

Degenerate and inverted elements are inevitable when an object performs large deformations (e.g., under heavy compression or by overstretching). However, constitutive models are meaningful only for regular deformations. Moreover, the wrongly deformed elements would cause numerical instability, even leading to simulation failure. An example is shown in Fig. 1.8 (Top): a model is over-stretched, causing unstable deformation behaviors.

Stress-Based Extension

An invertible FEM model (IFEM) was proposed by Irving et al. [44, 45]. The deformation gradient $F \in \mathbb{R}^{3 \times 3}$ is used to detect whether an element is inverted, by checking the sign of its determinant. An inverted element is corrected by modifying the components of *SVD* decomposition of *F*. Meanwhile, a *modified neo-Hookean* material model was proposed to avoid extremely large stiffness under heavy compression. However, an explicit integration scheme was used here that required stringent restriction of time-step size. To alleviate this problem, an implicit time integration was formulated by Teran et al. [46]. By manipulating element stiffness

Fig. 1.8 *Top* unstable deformations caused by inverted elements; *Bottom* stable performance by a constitutive model with an energetically-based extension [43]

matrices, a positive-definiteness global Hessian matrix (i.e., the tangent stiffness matrix) was formulated to ensure numerical stability. Sin et al. [47] proposed an alternative method to compute the tangent stiffness matrix, which works on *constitutive models* defined by *principal stretches*, instead of the *invariants* based models as in [46].

Energetically-Based Extension
Modified constitutive models lose certain accuracy under extreme deformations. However, this trade-off for stability and visual plausibility is acceptable. In the aforementioned papers, modifications with constitutive models are *stress based*. An *energetically-based extension* was recently proposed by Stomakhin et al. [43]. A stable simulation under large stretching deformations is shown in Fig. 1.8 (Bottom). The *primary contour* of a strain energy density function is used to analyze the robustness and stability of a constitutive model. A *smooth energy extension of* a constitutive model is formulated to get a favorable primary contour, and it is more robust than stress-based extensions.

1.3.1.3 Large Time Steps

Implicit Time Integration
Explicit integration schemes are quite efficient for solving the system of equations of motion; however, they are only *conditionally stable*, meaning that the time-step sizes must be sufficiently small to ensure numerical stability, which limits their usage in practical applications. In contrast, implicit integrators are unconditionally stable but computationally much more expensive. Due to their stability with large time steps and large stiffnesses, they are popular in practical applications. A prominent work using an implicit integration scheme was proposed by Baraff et al. [31] for cloth simulation. Implementations of an implicit Euler integrator and an implicit *Newmark* integrator [48] can be found in the Vega FEM library [49].

1.3.2 Efficiency-Concerned Models

Rigorous *nonlinear* constitutive models can produce physically accurate results, but expensive computations become a bottleneck for performance. Especially, it is not practical to use these nonlinear models in real-time or interactive applications. There is always trade-off between accuracy and speed in graphics applications. In this section, we discuss various approaches that were proposed to speed up the performance of dynamics simulation.

1.3.2.1 Optimization Implicit Euler

For nonlinear elastic models, large systems of nonlinear equations are produced with implicit integration, which are often solved by *Newton's method* or its variations. However, convergence behavior of Newton's method is unreliable at large time steps, particularly for stiff systems. Recasting the implicit Euler integration as a minimization problem allows the Newton's method to be stabilized by more robust optimization strategies [50]. Though essentially the same equations are solved, an optimization solver can be more robust and efficient. This approach recently gains popularity in graphics community [8, 9, 51–55].

With a specially designed energy function, an alternating optimization scheme was used in [8, 9]. It guarantees convergence and makes safeguards as in Newton's method unnecessary. Furthermore, in their formulations the global system matrix is constant thus it can be pre-factored, resulting in a much more efficient solver than using implicit integrators.

1.3.2.2 Simplified Constitutive Models

For applications not requiring physically accurate results, simplified constitutive models (i.e., strain energy density functions) can be devised, which reduce cost related to computations of internal forces, tangent stiffness matrix, etc.

These simplified energy functions are geometrically motivated or simplified continuum-based constitutive models, which often have intuitive meanings for tuning material properties. For instance, in the seminal work of Terzopoulos et al. [37], the elastic models actually do not follow constitutive models as in continuum mechanics, but are formulated based on the *fundamental forms* of a parametric geometric shape (curve, surface, or solid). Teschner et al. [32] formulated a simple constraint based energy: a constraint of the form $C(x_0, \ldots, x_{n-1})$ is defined for the preservation of length, surface area or volume, based on which a potential energy can be formulated as $E = \frac{1}{2}kC^2$, where k is the stiffness of the constraint. Then the corresponding internal forces can be computed as $f_i = -\frac{\partial E}{\partial x_i}$, and the stiffness matrix K as $K_{ij} = \frac{\partial^2 E}{\partial x_i \partial x_j}$. Huang et al. [56] presented a potential energy in terms of the L^2 norm of the change of the *differential coordinates*, which was inspired by mesh editing methods [4, 5, 57] discussed in Sect. 1.1.1; the corresponding stiffness matrix is approximately constant, which enables fast and stable implicit time integration. In [51, 58], a simplified *St. Venant-Kirchhoff* material model was used to reduce computation.

1.3.2.3   Model Reduction Methods

Model reduction methods (also known as *subspace methods*) reduce computational complexity by decreasing the system DOF of dynamics simulation. The idea is that a full DOF deformation space is approximated by a subspace spanned by a small number of *modes* (i.e., the *subspace basis*).

Suppose that a number of r vectors ($\in \mathbb{R}^{3n}$) are already obtained as the subspace basis, and are assembled by columns into a *modal matrix* $U \in \mathbb{R}^{3n \times r}$, where n is the number of vertices of a volumetric mesh. The full DOF displacement vector $u \in \mathbb{R}^{3n}$ is projected into the subspace spanned by the column vectors of U, and we have $u = Uq$, where $q \in \mathbb{R}^r$ is called *modal coordinates*. Therefore, the original full DOF equations of motion $M\ddot{u} + D\dot{u} + f_{int}(u) = f_{ext}$ (refer to Sect. 3.4.1) become a reduced system with DOF of r, as

$$U^T M U \ddot{q} + U^T D U \dot{q} + U^T f_{int}(Uq) = U^T f_{ext},$$

where $M \in \mathbb{R}^{3n \times 3n}$ is the mass matrix, $D \in \mathbb{R}^{3n \times 3n}$ the damping matrix, and $f_{int} \in \mathbb{R}^{3n}$ and $f_{ext} \in \mathbb{R}^{3n}$ are internal and external forces respectively. Therefore, instead of solving a system with full DOF unknowns, only r unknowns need to solved, where $r \ll 3n$.

Various subspace basis generation methods are discussed below.

Linear Modal Analysis
A common way of generating deformation modes is to use *linear modal analysis* (LMA) [59, 60]. Pentland et al. [61] pioneered the use of LMA in graphics: given the mass matrix M and the system stiffness matrix K, a generalized eigen-value problem $Kx = \lambda Mx$ is solved. The eigenvectors are called *vibration modes*, with *frequencies* equal to the roots of the corresponding eigenvalues. Only a small number of modes with *low frequencies* need to be pre-computed, which are used to approximate the full space of deformations. Figure 1.9 shows ten linear modes with low frequencies of a dino model, with its feet fixed in positions.

An interactive reduced simulation with LMA was presented by Hauser et al. [62]. With pre-computed linear modes and Rayleigh damping, they showed that the system of motion equations could be *decoupled* into a set of second-order differential equations, which could be solved independently and efficiently.

The advantages of using linear modes are that the linear modes can be pre-computed efficiently (using math libraries such as *ARPACK* [63]), and that simulation complexity only depends on the number of modes and is independent of the

Fig. 1.9 Ten linear models of the a constrained dino model (with its feet fixed in positions)

complexity of the simulated mesh. Real-time performance can be achieved, which is useful in interactive applications. However, since only linear modes are used, noticeable artifacts would occur for large deformations, such as volume distortion (similar to the artifacts caused by the linear FEM model) and locking artifacts [64] (also known as *artificial stiffening*, meaning that deformations are constrained to a limited range, even if large external loads are applied).

Modal Derivatives

To support large deformations with subspace methods, Barbič et al. [65] proposed a *modal derivatives* method for generating nonlinear subspace basis. A combination of linear modes and *tangent linear vibration modes* are shown in Fig. 1.10.

Fig. 1.10 Linear modes Ψ^i and mass-normalized modal derivates $\overline{\Phi}^{ij}$ [65]

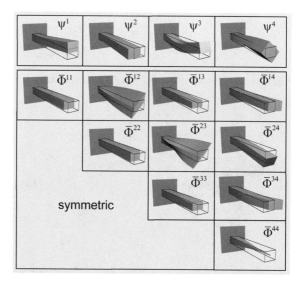

The formulation is based on a particular *St. Venant-Kirchhoff* (StVK) material. With r linear modes, $r * (r + 1)/2$ modal derivatives are computed, and the final low-dimensional deformation basis is obtained by applying *mass-PCA* on a total number of $(r + r * (r + 1)/2)$ modes. The generated modes of the dino model are shown in Fig. 1.11: Mass-PCA is applied on a combination of 10 linear modes and 55 modal derivatives, and the first 10 modes are shown here.

For comparison, we show the deformations generated by a full DOF model, the modal derivatives method and the LMA method respectively in Fig. 1.12. It shows that the modal derivatives method (Fig. 1.12b) can generate deformations comparable to a full DOF simulation (Fig. 1.12a), but the LMA method exhibits a *stiffening* artifact (Fig. 1.12c).

Modal Warping

The modal derivatives method with the StVK material can generate physically-plausible results, but it cannot be easily extended to other constitutive models. Tycowicz et al. [66] proposed a simple extension by changing components of the linear modes. Choi et al. [67] proposed a *modal warping* method for large deformations, eliminating distortions caused by linear modes through extrapolating

Fig. 1.11 By applying mass-PCA on 65 combined modes, the first ten modes are shown here

(a)   (b)   (c)

Fig. 1.12 a Full simulation; **b** modal derivatives method; **c** linear modes

element rotations (similar to the idea of stiffness warping). Huang et al. [68] proposed a warping method based on *Rotation-Strain coordinates* (RS), which corrected the distortions of linear modes by post processing. This method was also employed in a deformation editing system [69]. Li et al. [70] extended this RS concept to a reduced RS space to further improve performance.

Neither of the modal warping method nor the RS method is physically correct, but both of them can produce visually-plausible results with only linear modes.

Considering Local Deformations
Subspace methods greatly reduce computational cost; however, the subspace basis only has global support such that local deformation details can hardly be captured. One practical solution is to decompose a simulated object into a number of small subdomains, which is known as a *multi-domain* approach. Barbič et al. [71] presented a deformable model with articulated tree-structured subdomains, which are connected by small or nearly rigid interfaces. Kim et al. [72] employed the subspace techniques in physically-based skinning, where a character is decomposed according to its bone structures. The inter-domain interfaces can be large, and the subdomains are coupled using penalty forces (soft constraints) to avoid crack artifact. Yang et al. [73] improved the coupling constraints to avoid over-constraint problem. A more physically accurate method [74] is to compute local deformation basis from the *analytic* solutions of a *static loading problem*, but it costs much more than the former multi-domain methods.

Notes and Remarks
Compared with full DOF simulation methods, subspace techniques can greatly reduce computational complexity. By trading accuracy for speed, they can be applied to interactive applications that require only visual plausibility. Note that since the subspace basis is pre-computed, topology of the simulated mesh should not be changed (e.g., no fracturing) during simulation. The subspace concept is also employed for shape analysis and shape editing [75–78], where eigen values and eigen vectors (also called *spectra*, or *eigen modes*) of a Hessian matrix of a discrete surface energy are analyzed.

1.3.2.4 Cubature Schemes

Reduced internal forces in the former subspace methods are evaluated, either by computing full DOF internal forces (at high computational cost) and projecting to a subspace by $U^T f_{int}$, or by a particular formulation of the StVK material with complexity of $O(r^4)$ [65]. An et al. [79] proposed a *cubature* scheme (as an extension of *Gaussian quadrature* scheme) for efficiently integrating reduced internal forces at a cost of $O(r^2)$ for $O(r)$ cubature points. This scheme is successfully applied in real-time applications, such as physically-based characters skinning [72] and deformation editing [70].

1.3.2.5 Generalized Continuum-Based Models

Frame-Based Elastic Models
Jumping out of rigorous physics-thinking, Gilles et al. [80, 81] proposed a new deformable model that combines concepts of continuum mechanics and frame-based skinning techniques (such as *linear blending* and *dual-quaternion blending*) used in skeletal animation. As shown in Fig. 1.13, a sparse set of frames is distributed inside a mesh object. The DOF required to be solved are the low dimensional coordinate frames, instead of the mesh nodes as in previous FEM discretization. Based on continuum mechanics, mechanical quantities (such as mass matrix, internal forces and stiffness matrix) are generalized to be formulated in terms of the DOF of the frames. The equations of motion are also reformulated, yielding a system of rather small dimensions. Dynamics motion of the frames is computed, and finally the coupled mesh is deformed by a skinning method.

One advantage of this method is that local deformations can be supported by inserting new frames on-the-fly. More follow-up works can be found in [82–84].

Rig-Space Physics
Similar in spirit with the frame-based generalization, Hahn et al. [85, 86] further generalized the formulation in a rig-space for a rigged character, which unifies physics simulation and keyframing. The output consists of animation curves. It is useful in animation design, which provides artists with intuitive control of mechanical behaviors through high-level rig parameters, and meanwhile automatically produces secondary dynamic motions.

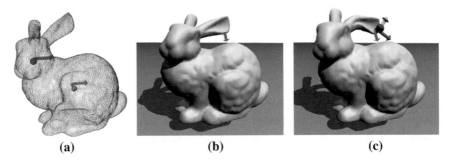

(a)   (b)   (c)

Fig. 1.13 Frame-based deformable model. Two frames are able to model a deformable body. *Left* Besides material properties, flexibility of the simulated object also depends on the distribution of frames: by inserting a new frame at one ear *Right*, the ear becomes more flexible than the previous one *Middle* [80]

1.4   Hybrid Models: Bridging the Gap Between Geometrical and Physical Models

Geometrically-based and physically-based deformable models are not totally disconnected from each other, but to some extent closely related. The aforementioned elastic models proposed by Terzopoulos et al. [37] are a typical example. Chao et al. [13] provided a proof of the relationship between a geometric model and a *Biot strain* based model. In this section, we discuss some hybrid models that benefit from both groups: they take advantage of the stability and efficiency of geometrical models, while still having continuum-based foundation.

1.4.1 Continuum-Based Constraints Within a PBD Framework

In the original PBD framework as discussed in Sect. 1.1.2.2 geometric constraints are used. Limitations with geometric constraints are that deformation behaviors depend on the tessellation (or, discretization) of a simulated object, and material properties are defined in terms of constraint stiffnesses.

Recently, Müller et al. [87] presented a strain-based constraint defined on the entries of the rotation-invariant *Green strain tensor*. *Anisotropic* material properties can be defined in terms of the stiffnesses of stretches and shears along different material directions. Similar in spirit, [88] used a *continuum-based energy* as a constraint, such as the potential energy of the StVK material or the *Neo-Hookean* material.

This kind of continuum-based formulations does not suffer from the tessellation bias problem, and provides continuum mechanics support for the PBD framework.

1.4.2 Continuum-Based Constraints Within an Optimization Framework

Bouaziz et al. [9] proposed a *projective dynamics* approach that recasts implicit Euler integration to an optimization problem as discussed in Sect. 1.3.1.3. It generalizes the *local/global optimization scheme* from a mass-spring system [8] to the FEM methods. Various constraints are supported, including both geometric constraints (e.g., [89]) and continuum-based constraints. With a specially designed continuum-based energy function that includes additional auxiliary variables, the connection between PBD and FEM methods is further analyzed.

1.5   Control Methods of Deformable Models

We have introduced various methods for dynamics simulation of deformable models. However, this is only part of the story. In graphics applications, *deformation control* is also much desired but it poses challenges, such as stable intuitive adjustment of material properties, and interactive control over complex mechanical behaviors. In this section, we discuss several methods related to deformation control.

1.5.1   Example-Based Methods

In computer animations, dynamics simulation relieves artists of laborious keyframing for modeling dynamic behaviors of deformable objects. Secondary dynamic motions like jiggling effects can be obtained automatically. However, deformations produced by simulation are not always what an artist wants, and it is often very difficult or impractical to tune the material properties of a complex model in order to obtain the desired deformations.

Usually, an artist has a notion on how a deformable object should be deformed in a certain scenario. Motivated by this requirement, Martin et al. [51] proposed an *example-based method*, which takes some pre-designed example poses as input and generates deformations complied with these examples, as shown in Fig. 1.14. The idea is that an example space spanned by the example poses is used to derive an *example-based potential*, from which attractive forces are derived to project a deformed configuration into the example space. Schumacher et al. [90] improved the efficiency of this method by using incompatible rest shapes. Koyama et al. [17] applied this idea within a *shape matching* framework to achieve real-time performance. Zhang et al. [91] proposed a real-time integration method in a reduced subspace, where the example poses are included to form a subspace basis.

Example-based methods provide artistic control over complex deformation behaviors without manipulating complicated material properties, though the artificial forces induced by the example-based potential affect physical accuracy. A limitation is that the deformation behaviors might not be predictable if too many

Fig. 1.14 Example-based deformations [51]. Deformations are artistically controlled by various example poses

example poses are provided, this leads to the question of how many examples should be designed to achieve both complex and *directable* deformations.

1.5.2 Space-Time Control

Space-time control method is used for editing elastic object animation. It is formulated as an optimization problem: existing animation sequences are edited through position constraints, then an optimization procedure seeks *optimal control forces* (i.e., least amount of non-physical/artificial forces) to match the input spatial constraints in time.

Barbič et al. [92] used a time-varying *linear quadratic regulator* to drive an object to follow pre-defined trajectories. Later, a *reduced space-time optimization* method [93] was proposed to enforce a deformable object to follow a sparse set of pre-designed keyframes. Furthermore, an interactive animation editor [69] was presented: some keyframes of an existing animation are edited, then the whole animation is reproduced, respecting both physics and user preference. Recently, Li et al. [70] proposed a space-time editing scheme that optimizes not only control forces but also material properties to better match user defined constraints.

Instead of optimizing control forces or material properties, Coros et al. [58] proposed a *rest shape adaption method*. It dynamically changes the rest shape of a deformable object during simulation. In order to satisfy a user-defined *locomotion goal* (e.g., position and velocity of the center-of-mass of an object) at a certain time step, the rest shape is adapted such that a new deformed shape propels itself through interactions with the environment (e.g., collision and friction). It makes a deformable object acts like a living creature, in a self-propelled way that changes its shape through internal forces instead of external artificial forces. However, this method is limited to a planning horizon of one time step, and can be difficult to generate meaningful motions for a complex model in a long time range rather than a single time step.

1.6   Main Research Issues

Deformable object modeling has been an active research topic in computer graphics [24, 38–40]. Since it was introduced to the graphics community in the late 1980s [37], many works with various modeling approaches have been published.

We have briefly introduced the fundamental issues on simulation of deformable models. As can been seen in the above sections, researchers have focused on visually realistic physical simulations of the motion and properties of deformable objects. Different from rigid body simulation, the shape of deformable objects can change due to external impacts with an infinite number of degrees-of-freedom. The scope of deformable objects is large, including objects of different dimensions, such as 1D ropes and hairs, 2D shells and cloths, and 3D solids such as animal organs.

Various approaches, which have their own advantages and limitations, have been analyzed. This chapter is devoted to continuum-based approaches in combination with the finite element method. Other related topics such as fracture [94], and collision detection and response [95, 96] are beyond this survey, thus they are not covered here.

The ability to model and manipulate deformable objects is essential to many applications, such as geometry modeling and processing in computer aided design, animations, computer games, virtual reality, visual effects industries. Although the computational power of modern computers is increasing, there are still a lot of challenges to achieve deformable models with more physical realism, stability and controllability. We are quite interested in this topic, and make an effort to push the technologies to further development.

Besides computational *accuracy*, computer graphics applications often have their own challenges as follows:

- *Stability*—Large deformations caused by strong external impacts are common in graphics applications, where degenerate and inverted deformations would occur, causing numerical instability or even failure of the simulation. Relatively large time step size, which is desirable for simulation efficiency, can also lead to convergence problem. Therefore, robust algorithms with guaranteed convergence are required for a simulation to be used in a practical application.
- *Efficiency*—In contrast to dynamics simulation of rigid bodies that only involves a few degrees-of-freedom (DOF), a deformable object usually contains a large number of DOF, which leads to the need to solve large systems of equations. Both computation and memory intensive solvers are commonly required. However, there is usually a strictly limited budget of computing resources for the simulation phase in an application, especially in real-time or interactive applications such as games or virtual surgery applications. Therefore, an efficient solver with fast convergence rate plays a critical role. Computation reduction and approximation strategies are also desirable for performance improvement.
- *Controllability*—Deformation control is an important concern for many graphics applications. For example, in animation design, instead of passively accepting the results automatically generated by a simulation, artists would often require intuitive and stable controls over the material properties and animation behaviors in order to realize artistic or creative motions; in other words, to have *directable* deformations. Deformation behaviors can be controlled by stable adjusting material parameters, or by adding artificial forces of least interference with physical authenticity, etc. This kind of controllability should be intuitive and easy for user interactions.
- *Accuracy* also plays an *important* role here. However, without infinite computing resources, there are always trade-offs, and a proper solution is to seek good compromise among these criteria. For example, in computer games, stable

and fast responses are of greater importance than physical accuracy, thus certain accuracy has to be sacrificed for efficiency and stability; in animation design, controllability is desirable for artistic designs with a slight loss of accuracy; in graphics industries such as film production, efficient algorithms would save expenses in terms of time and money. In these cases, only visual plausibility in terms of accuracy is required if physical accuracy is expensive to achieve.

We mainly work on physically-based deformable models. The mathematical models are continuum-based rather than geometrically motivated. In contrast to existing research that mainly works on isotropic materials, we focus on complex anisotropic materials that commonly exist in the real world.

Anisotropic materials have been less studied in the field of computer graphics, and most of the publications focus on modeling of isotropic materials. Due to the computational complexity of anisotropic deformations, anisotropic materials are rarely used in practical applications; moreover, there is lack of ways to control anisotropic mechanical properties.

We investigate the formulation for deformable models of anisotropic materials, and design interactive tools for intuitive control of anisotropic deformation behaviors. Our proposed methods add no computational cost during simulation, with the help of precomputation.

Furthermore, based on the observation that many real-world soft objects, such as the skins and soft tissues of animal and human characters, are linked to rigid skeletons, we also consider augmenting skeleton control with deformable objects, and finally develop a skeletal animation system that encompasses all these techniques.

With their computational efficiency and stability, our methods have a great potential to be used in many real-time applications, such as virtual surgery and animations, with improved physical realism.

There are some helpful open source libraries worth mentioning. We began with the *OpenCloth* library [97] that is simple and easy-to-follow. It includes cloth simulation, the corotational FEM model and various time integrators. The *Vega FEM* library [98] has implemented several physically based deformable models, and provided useful data structures and linear algebra algorithms. The *SOFA* framework [99], which includes GPU implementations, primarily targets at real-time medical simulation for soft tissues. There are also some open source physics engines that support deformable models, such as *Bullet physics engine* [20], which is a professional 3D real-time multi-physics library.

1.7 Organization of the Chapters

In this chapter, we discuss and analyze various approaches including geometrical models, physically-based models, hybrid models, and deformation control methods. Our focus is on physically-based approaches, which build a foundation for our work. We then give a brief introduction of the research problems, and describe the research background, challenges and our objectives.

Chapter 2 is an introduction to the representation of deformable models. The previously developed *isosurface stuffing* algorithm fills an isosurface with a uniformly sized tetrahedral mesh. The algorithm is fast and numerically robust. It generates tetrahedra from a small set of precomputed stencils. A variant of the algorithm creates a mesh with internal grading.

Chapter 3 provides fundamental theories on continuum-based deformable models, including elasticity theory, finite element discretization, dynamics equations of motion and numerical integration schemes.

Chapter 4 presents dynamics simulation of transversely isotropic deformable objects. We propose a fiber-field incorporated FEM model for deformation control, which is our first effort on simulation of anisotropic materials.

Chapter 5 further investigates orthotropic materials. We develop a frame-field augmented FEM model for dynamics simulation of orthotropic deformable objects. A Laplacian smoothing method is developed to generate a frame-field for an orthotropic model. An interactive approach for deformation control is presented.

Chapter 6 extends our research to skeletal character animation. We combine continuum-based models with position-based dynamics, and incorporate skeleton control into deformable character animation. Finally, we design a skeletal character animation system that can generate physically-plausible dynamic motions of soft tissues with stable and efficient performance.

Chapter 7 concludes our work and discusses potential research issues in the future.

References

1. Botsch, M., et al. (2010). *Polygon mesh processing*. CRC press.
2. Crane, K., et al. (2013). Digital geometry processing with discrete exterior calculus. In *ACM SIGGRAPH 2013 courses*. ACM.
3. Panozzo, D., & Jacobson, A. (2015). *Libigl tutorial notes*. SGP Graduate School 2015.
4. Sorkine, O., & Alexa, M. (2007). As-rigid-as-possible surface modeling. In *Symposium on geometry processing*.
5. Sorkine, O., et al. (2004). Laplacian surface editing. In *Proceedings of the 2004 eurographics/ACM SIGGRAPH symposium on geometry processing*. ACM.
6. Zhang, S., Huang, J., & Metaxas, D. N. (2011). Robust mesh editing using Laplacian coordinates. *Graphical Models, 73*(1), 10–19.
7. Zhou, K., et al. (2005). Large mesh deformation using the volumetric graph laplacian. In *ACM transactions on graphics (TOG)*. ACM.
8. Liu, T., et al. (2013). Fast simulation of mass-spring systems. *ACM Transactions on Graphics (TOG), 32*(6), 214.
9. Bouaziz, S., et al. (2014). Projective dynamics: Fusing constraint projections for fast simulation. *ACM Transactions on Graphics (TOG), 33*(4), 154.
10. Müller, M., et al. (2005). Meshless deformations based on shape matching. In *ACM transactions on graphics (TOG)*. ACM.

11. Müller, M., et al. (2002). Stable real-time deformations. In *Proceedings of the 2002 ACM SIGGRAPH/eurographics symposium on computer animation*. ACM.
12. Müller, M., & Gross, M. (2004). Interactive virtual materials. In *Proceedings of graphics interface* (pp. 239–246). Canadian Human-Computer Communications Society: London, Ontario, Canada.
13. Chao, I., et al. (2010). A simple geometric model for elastic deformations. In *ACM transactions on graphics (TOG)*. ACM.
14. Jakobsen, T. (2001). Advanced character physics. In *Game developers conference*.
15. Rivers, A. R., & James, D. L. (2007). FastLSM: Fast lattice shape matching for robust real-time deformation. *ACM Transactions on Graphics, 26*(3), 82.
16. Steinemann, D., Otaduy, M. A. & Gross, M. (2008). Fast adaptive shape matching deformations. In *Proceedings of the 2008 ACM SIGGRAPH/eurographics symposium on computer animation* (pp. 87–94). Eurographics Association: Dublin, Ireland.
17. Koyama, Y., et al. (2012). Real-time example-based elastic deformation. In *Proceedings of the 11th ACM SIGGRAPH/eurographics conference on computer animation*. Eurographics Association.
18. Müller, M., & Chentanez, N. (2011). Solid simulation with oriented particles. *ACM Transactions on Graphics (TOG), 30*(4), 92.
19. Bender, J., Müller, M., & Macklin, M. (2015). Position-based simulation methods in computer graphics. In *Tutorial proceedings of eurographics*.
20. Coumans, E. (2010). *Bullet physics engine*. Open Source Software: http://bulletphysics.org 1.
21. Müller, M., et al. (2007). Position based dynamics. *Journal of Visual Communication and Image Representation, 18*(2), 109–118.
22. Micky Kelager, S. N., & Erleben, K. (2010). A triangle bending constraint model for position-based dynamics. In *Proceedings of VRIPHYS'2010* (pp. 31–37).
23. Diziol, R., Bender, J., & Bayer, D. (2011). Robust real-time deformation of incompressible surface meshes. In *Proceedings of the 2011 ACM SIGGRAPH/eurographics symposium on computer animation* (pp. 237–246). ACM: Vancouver, British Columbia, Canada.
24. Müller, M., et al. (2008). Real time physics: class notes. In *ACM SIGGRAPH 2008 classes* (pp. 1–90). ACM: Los Angeles, California.
25. Bender, J., et al. (2014). A survey on position-based simulation methods in computer graphics. *Computer Graphics Forum, 33*(6), 228–251.
26. Mollemans, W., et al. (2003). Tetrahedral mass spring model for fast soft tissue deformation. In N. Ayache & H. Delingette (Eds.), *Surgery simulation and soft tissue modeling, proceedings* (pp. 145–154).
27. Halic, T., et al. (2009). Soft tissue deformation and optimized data structures for mass spring methods. In *Bioinformatics and bioengineering. Ninth IEEE international conference on BIBE '09* 2009.
28. Selle, A., Lentine, M., & Fedkiw, R. (2008). A mass spring model for hair simulation. *ACM Transactions on Graphics, 27*(3), 1–11.
29. San-Vicente, G., Aguinaga, I., & Celigueta, J. T. (2012). Cubical mass-spring model design based on a tensile deformation test and nonlinear material model. *IEEE Transactions on Visualization and Computer Graphics, 18*(2), 228–241.
30. Tu, X. (1999). *Artificial animals for computer animation: biomechanics, locomotion, perception, and behavior*. Springer Science & Business Media.
31. Baraff, D., & Witkin, A. (1998). Large steps in cloth simulation. In *Proceedings of the 25th annual conference on Computer graphics and interactive techniques* (pp. 43–54). ACM.
32. Teschner, M., et al. (2004). A versatile and robust model for geometrically complex deformable solids. In *CGI '04: proceedings of the computer graphics international*. IEEE Computer Society.
33. Ward, J. P. (1992). *Solid mechanics: an introduction* (Vol 15). Springer Science & Business Media.

34. Kelly, P., Solid mechanics lecture notes. http://homepages.engineering.auckland.ac.nz/ ~pkel015/SolidMechanicsBooks/index.html: Department of Engineering Science, University of Auckland.
35. Cook, R. D. (2007). *Concepts and applications of finite element analysis*. Wiley.
36. Bonet, J., & Wood, R. D. (2008). *Nonlinear continuum mechanics for finite element analysis* (2nd ed.). Cambridge university press.
37. Terzopoulos, D., et al. (1987). Elastically deformable models. *SIGGRAPH Computer Graphics, 21*(4), 205–214.
38. Gibson, S. F. F., & Mirtich, B. (1997). *A survey of deformable modeling in computer graphics*. Technical Report TR-97-1, 1997. 9.
39. Nealen, A., et al. (2006). Physically based deformable models in computer graphics. *Computer Graphics Forum, 25*(4), 809–836.
40. Sifakis, E., & Barbic, J. (2012). FEM simulation of 3D deformable solids: a practitioner's guide to theory, discretization and model reduction. In *ACM SIGGRAPH 2012 courses*. ACM.
41. Allard, J., Courtecuisse, H., & Faure, F. (2011). Implicit FEM solver on GPU for interactive deformation simulation. In W. H. Wen-mei (Ed.), *GPU computing gems Jade Edition* (pp. 281–294), Elsevier.
42. Georgii, J., & Westermann, R. (2008). Corotated finite elements made fast and stable. *VRIPHYS, 8,* 11–19.
43. Stomakhin, A., et al. (2012). Energetically consistent invertible elasticity. In *Eurographics/ACM SIGGRAPH symposium on computer animation*. The Eurographics Association.
44. Irving, G., J. Teran, & Fedkiw, R. (2004). Invertible finite elements for robust simulation of large deformation. In *Proceedings of the 2004 ACM SIGGRAPH/eurographics symposium on computer animation* (pp. 131–140). Eurographics Association: Grenoble, France.
45. Irving, G., Teran, J., & Fedkiw, R. (2006). Tetrahedral and hexahedral invertible finite elements. *Graphical Models, 68*(2), 66–89.
46. Teran, J., et al. (2005). Robust quasistatic finite elements and flesh simulation. In *Proceedings of the 2005 ACM SIGGRAPH/eurographics symposium on computer animation* (pp. 181–190). ACM: Los Angeles, California.
47. Sin, F., et al. (2011). Invertible isotropic hyperelasticity using SVD gradients. In *Posters and demos, 2011 ACM SIGGRAPH/eurographics symposium on computer animation* 2011.
48. Wriggers, P., & Laursen, T. A. (2006). *Computational contact mechanics* (Vol 30167). Springer.
49. Jernej, B., Fun, S. S., & Daniel, S. (2012). *Vega FEM library*. http://www.jernejbarbic.com/vega
50. Nocedal, J., & Wright, S. (2006). *Numerical optimization*. Springer Science & Business Media.
51. Martin, S., et al. (2011). Example-based elastic materials. *ACM Transactions on Graphics (TOG), 30*(4), 72.
52. Gast, T. F., & Schroeder, C. (2014). Optimization integrator for large time steps. In *Proceedings of the ACM SIGGRAPH/eurographics symposium on computer animation* (pp. 31–40). Eurographics Association: Copenhagen, Denmark.
53. Frâncu, M., & Moldoveanu, F. (2015). Cloth simulation using soft constraints. *Journal of WSCG (Cumulative issue), 23*(1–3), pp. 9–18. ISBN 978-80-86943-64-0.
54. Kharevych, L., et al. (2006). Geometric, variational integrators for computer animation. In *Proceedings of the 2006 ACM SIGGRAPH/eurographics symposium on computer animation*. Eurographics Association.
55. Deng, B., et al. (2015). Interactive design exploration for constrained meshes. *Computer-Aided Design, 61,* 13–23.
56. Huang, J., et al. (2006). Geometrically based potential energy for simulating deformable objects. *The Visual Computer, 22*(9–11), 740–748.

57. Alexa, M. (2003). Differential coordinates for local mesh morphing and deformation. *The Visual Computer, 19*(2), 105–114.
58. Coros, S., et al. (2012). Deformable objects alive! *ACM Transactions on Graphics (TOG), 31* (4), p. 69.
59. Shabana, A. A. (1996). *Theory of vibration: an introduction* (Vol. 1). Springer.
60. Hunter, P., & Pullan, A. (2001). *Fem/bem notes*. Department of Engineering Science: The University of Auckland, New Zeland.
61. Pentland, A., & Williams, J. (1989). Good vibrations: Modal dynamics for graphics and animation. *SIGGRAPH Computer Graphics, 23*(3), 207–214.
62. Hauser, K. K., Shen, C., & O'Brien, J. F. (2003). Interactive deformation using modal analysis with constraints. In *Graphics interface*.
63. Lehoucq, R. B., Sorensen, D. C., & Yang, C. (1998). *ARPACK users' guide: solution of large-scale eigenvalue problems with implicitly restarted Arnoldi methods* (Vol. 6). Siam.
64. Barbič, J. (2007). *Real-time reduced large-deformation models and distributed contact for computer graphics and haptics*. Carnegie Mellon University.
65. Barbič, J., & James, D. L. (2005). Real-time subspace integration for St. Venant-Kirchhoff deformable models. In *ACM SIGGRAPH 2005 papers* (pp. 982–990). ACM: Los Angeles, California.
66. von Tycowicz, C., et al. (2013). An efficient construction of reduced deformable objects. *ACM Transactions on Graphics (TOG), 32*(6), 213.
67. Choi, M. G., & Ko, H.-S. (2005). Modal warping: Real-time simulation of large rotational deformation and manipulation. *IEEE Transactions on Visualization and Computer Graphics, 11*(1), 91–101.
68. Huang, J., et al. (2011). Interactive shape interpolation through controllable dynamic deformation. *IEEE Transactions on Visualization and Computer Graphics, 17*(7), 983–992.
69. Barbič, J., Sin, F., & Grinspun, E. (2012). Interactive editing of deformable simulations. *ACM Transaction on Graphics (SIGGRAPH 2012), 31*(4).
70. Li, S., et al. (2014). Space-time editing of elastic motion through material optimization and reduction. *ACM Transactions on Graphics, 33*(4) p. Art. No. 108.
71. Barbič, J., & Zhao, Y. (2011). Real-time large-deformation substructuring. In *ACM SIGGRAPH 2011 papers* (pp. 1–8). ACM: Vancouver, British Columbia, Canada.
72. Kim, T., & James, D. L. (2011). Physics-based character skinning using multi-domain subspace deformations. In *Proceedings of the 2011 ACM SIGGRAPH/eurographics symposium on computer animation* (pp. 63–72). ACM: Vancouver, British Columbia, Canada.
73. Yang, Y., et al. (2013). Boundary-aware multi-domain subspace deformation. *IEEE Transactions on Visualization and Computer Graphics*.
74. Harmon, D., & Zorin, D. (2013). Subspace integration with local deformations. *ACM Transactions on Graphics (TOG), 32*(4), 107.
75. Hildebrandt, K., et al. (2011). Interactive surface modeling using modal analysis. *ACM Transactions on Graphics (TOG), 30*(5), 119.
76. Hildebrandt, K., et al. (2010). Eigenmodes of surface energies for shape analysis. In *Advances in geometric modeling and processing* (pp. 296–314). Springer.
77. Hildebrandt, K., et al. (2012). Modal shape analysis beyond Laplacian. *Computer Aided Geometric Design, 29*(5), 204–218.
78. von Tycowicz, C. (2014). *Concepts and algorithms for the deformation, analysis, and compression of digital shapes*. Freie Universität Berlin.
79. An, S. S., Kim, T. & James, D. L. (2008). Optimizing cubature for efficient integration of subspace deformations. In *ACM transactions on graphics (TOG)*. ACM.
80. Gilles, B., et al. (2011). Frame-based elastic models. *ACM Transactions on Graphics, 30*(2), 1–12.
81. Faure, F., et al. (2011). Sparse meshless models of complex deformable solids. *ACM Transactions on Graphics, 30*(4), 1–10.

82. Gilles, B., et al. (2013). Frame-based interactive simulation of complex deformable objects. In *Deformation models* (pp. 145–166). Springer.
83. Tournier, M., et al. (2014). Seamless adaptivity of elastic models. In *Proceedings of the 2014 graphics interface conference*. Canadian Information Processing Society.
84. Tournier, M., et al. (2014). Velocity-based adaptivity of deformable models. *Computers & Graphics, 45*, 75–85.
85. Hahn, F., et al. (2012). Rig-space physics. *ACM Transactions on Graphics, 31*(4), 1–8.
86. Hahn, F., et al. (2013). Efficient simulation of secondary motion in rig-space. In *Proceedings of the 12th ACM SIGGRAPH/eurographics symposium on computer animation* (pp. 165–171). ACM: Anaheim, California.
87. Müller, M., et al. (2014). Strain based dynamics. In *Proceedings of ACM SIGGRAPH/EUROGRAPHICS symposium on computer animation (SCA)*. Copenhagen.
88. Bender, J., et al. (2014). Position-based simulation of continuous materials. *Computers & Graphics, 44*, 1–10.
89. Bouaziz, S., et al. (2012). Shape-up: Shaping discrete geometry with projections. In *Computer graphics forum*. Wiley Online Library.
90. Schumacher, C., et al. (2012). Efficient simulation of example-based materials. In *Proceedings of the ACM SIGGRAPH/eurographics symposium on computer animation*. Eurographics Association.
91. Zhang, W., Zheng, J., & Thalmann, N. M. (2015). Real-time subspace integration for example-based elastic material. *Computer Graphics Forum, 34*(2), 395–404.
92. Barbič, J., & Popović, J. (2008). Real-time control of physically based simulations using gentle forces. In *ACM transactions on graphics (TOG)*. ACM.
93. Barbič, J., Silva, M. D., & Popović, J. (2009). Deformable object animation using reduced optimal control. *ACM Transactions on Graphics, 28*(3), 1–9.
94. Chen, Z., et al. (2014). Physics-inspired adaptive fracture refinement. *ACM Transactions on Graphics (TOG), 33*(4), 113.
95. Jiménez, P., Thomas, F., & Torras, C. (2001). 3D collision detection: a survey. *Computers & Graphics, 25*(2), 269–285.
96. Teschner, M., et al. (2005). Collision detection for deformable objects. In *Computer graphics forum*. Wiley Online Library.
97. Movania, M. M. (2011). *OpenCloth: A new open source cloth simulation library*. http://code.google.com/p/opencloth/
98. Jernej Barbič, F. S. S. (2012). Daniel Schroeder, *Vega FEM library*. http://www.jernejbarbic.com/vega
99. Allard, J., et al. (2007). SOFA—an open source framework for medical simulation. In J. D. Westwood, et al. (Eds.), *Medicine meets virtual reality 15* (pp. 13–18).

Chapter 2
Mesh Representation of Deformable Models

Abstract To prepare the ground for dynamics simulation with the Finite Element Method, we introduce a previously developed mesh representation algorithm, *isosurface stuffing*, which fills an object domain with a uniformly sized tetrahedral mesh. This algorithm generates tetrahedra from a small set of precomputed stencils. A variant of the algorithm creates a mesh with internal grading. That is, on the boundary where high resolution is desired, the tetrahedra elements are fine and uniformly sized; and in the interior, the tetrahedron may be coarser and vary in size.

2.1 Introduction

For the Finite Element Method (FEM) to be applied to a deformable model, the model should first be discretized into a mesh of elements. We choose tetrahedron as the mesh element for its topological simplicity and flexibility. Though the tetrahedral mesh generation algorithms can be based on the Delaunay triangulation, the latter is an iterative procedure and numerically sensitive in geometric calculations.

In this chapter, for simulations of the deformable structures such as human body, we introduce a more numerically robust algorithm termed *isosurface stuffing* [1]. Isosurface stuffing arises naturally in modeling with implicit surfaces. The input to the algorithm is a continuous *cut function* f: $R^3 \rightarrow R$ that implicitly represents the point set $\{p: f(p) \geq 0\}$ of the geometric domain to be stuffed with a tetrahedral mesh. The output is a tetrahedral mesh representing the geometrical model. The algorithm offers meaningful bounds on dihedral angles and conforms to the boundaries of geometric domains with complicated shapes.

2.2 Uniform Tetrahedral Mesh Generation

In the first phase, we fill a zero-surface ($f(p) = 0$) with uniformly sized tetrahedra in four steps.

© Springer International Publishing Switzerland 2016
J. Cai et al., *Graphical Simulation of Deformable Models*,
DOI 10.1007/978-3-319-51031-6_2

2.2.1 Generating the Body Centered Cubic Grid and Identical Tetrahedra

A space-tiling background grid is employed to guide the creation of a mesh. The *body centered cubic (BCC) lattice* is the union of two point grids:

$$BCC = Z^3 \cup (Z^3 + (1/2, 1/2, 1/2)),$$

where Z^3 is the grid of points with integer coordinates, and $Z^3 + (1/2, 1/2, 1/2)$ is a copy of that grid shifted to the center of each cube of the original grid.

As illustrated in Fig. 2.1, a space-filling tetrahedral mesh is defined by the *BCC grid* which is composed of identical tetrahedra with excellent quality, having edge lengths 1 and $\sqrt{3}/2$, and dihedral angles 60° and 90°.

For a general continuous cut function f, the first step is to find all the components of $f(p) = 0$. One way to find the points in P is to begin with several "seed" points known to be in the domain, and then find the rest by depth-first search on the edges of the BCC grid. Another way is to evaluate f at every lattice point in a user-specified bounding box.

We choose a subset P of the BCC lattice. P should include

  i. A lattice point p where the cut function $f(p) \geq 0$, and
 ii. A lattice point p of any $f(p)$ value, which is connected by an edge of the BCC grid to a lattice point where $f(p) > 0$

Then we compute and store the value of f at each lattice point in P.

2.2.2 Computing the Cut Points

The geometric modeler defines the cut function f and can handle a query for a point where a line segment intersects the zero-surface. One can do it by iterative

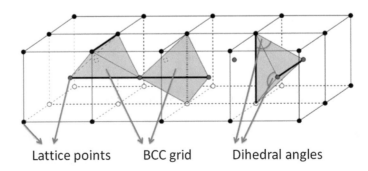

Lattice points   BCC grid   Dihedral angles

Fig. 2.1 The body centered cubic (BCC) lattice and three identical tetrahedra

Fig. 2.2 Computing or approximating the cut points

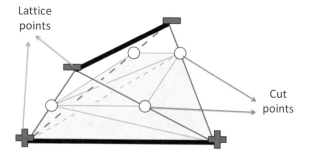

Lattice points

Cut points

bisection, which can approximate the cut point to a required accuracy. If f is expensive to evaluate, one could estimate the cut point by linear interpolation along the edge.

In details, for each edge of the BCC grid with both endpoints in P, if one endpoint is with $f > 0$ (inside) and the other is $f < 0$ (outside), we compute or approximate a *cut point* where the edge crosses the zero-surface, as illustrated in Fig. 2.2.

2.2.3 Warping the Background Grid

If a cut point c lies on a grid edge e, and the distance between c and an endpoint v of e is less than a certain threshold of the length of e, c is said to violate v. In this case, v is snapped to the isosurface, assigned a value of zero, and purged of adjoining cut points, *unless* the other endpoint of e gets snapped first, eliminating c.

In details, for each lattice point $q \in P$, check for the presence of cut points on the fourteen grid edges that adjoin q. If one of these cut points c is too close to q, we say that c *violates* q. If any cut point violates q, *warp* the grid by moving q to a cut point that violates q. We choose the nearest violating cut point, as illustrated in Fig. 2.3.

Technically, q is no longer a lattice point, but we still call it as such. The effect is to snap q onto the zero-surface and changing q's value to zero. We discard all cut points on the edges adjoining q, because those edges no longer have both a positive endpoint and a negative endpoint. Because we process every lattice point in P *sequentially* in this manner, no cut point adjoining q can subsequently cause another lattice point to move.

BCC grid edges come in two lengths, and we use a different value of α for each, chosen by experimentation. In practices, α_{long} is the coefficient for the longer, axis-aligned edges, which we call the *black edges*; and α_{short} is the coefficient for the shorter, diagonal edges, which we call the *red edges*. The order in which we process and warp the lattice points affects the final mesh, but it does not affect most

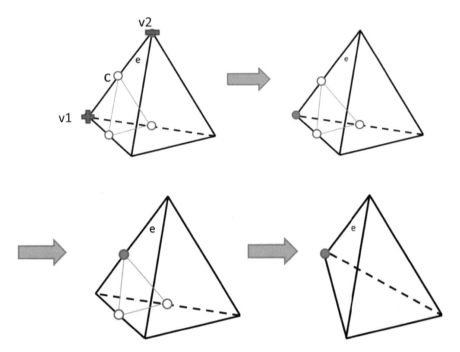

Fig. 2.3 Warp the grid $v1$ by moving it to a cut point c that violates $v1$

of our guarantees. The exceptions are wherein an angle bound is improved by *ordered warping*, in which we use the following algorithm to ensure that a lattice point never warps along an edge toward a neighboring vertex that will also be warped.

> **while** some negative lattice point $q-$ is violated by a cut point on an edge adjoining an *unviolated* positive lattice point.

Warp $q-$ to a violating cut point on such an edge;

> **while** some positive lattice point $q+$ is violated

Warp $q+$ to a violating cut point;

When this algorithm terminates, no violated lattice points survive, because if a negative lattice point is still violated when the first loop ends, the cut points that violate it are discarded when the second loop warps the violated positive lattice points.

2.2.4   Choosing Stencils for the Tetrahedral Mesh

For each BCC grid tetrahedron that has at least one vertex with a positive value, we fill the tetrahedron (which might be warped) with a stencil of 1–3 precomputed tetrahedra and output these tetrahedra. Figure 2.4 depicts the stencils. The choice of stencil depends on the signs of the four vertices of the BCC grid tetrahedron.

We store the stencils in a table, indexed by the signs of the vertex values (positive, negative, or zero). Some stencils generate two or three output tetrahedra, to respect surviving cut points on the grid edges. Symmetry reduces the number of distinct cases from 81 to the 12, as illustrated. In accounting for symmetry, note that black edges are not always interchangeable with red ones—some stencils offer better quality than others in particular circumstances, and not all stencils meet compatibly face-to-face. The seven stencils in the top row apply in all rotations and reflections, and their edges can be matched arbitrarily with the long and short edges of the BCC grid. For the remaining five stencils, the long edges of the BCC grid are depicted as thick and black; the short edges are red. For the three stencils in the bottom row (wherein the bottom long edge has both endpoints positive), the Parity Rule applies and may require a stencil to be reflected. The bottom five stencils apply in all rotations and reflections (left to right or front to back) that observe the Parity Rule and correctly match the edge colors.

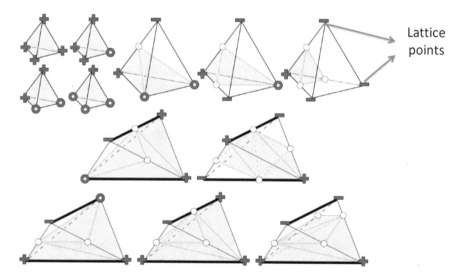

Fig. 2.4 Stencils for isosurface stuffing. Vertices of the BCC grid tetrahedra are labeled with their signs (+, −, 0). Cut points are *white*, and output tetrahedra are *yellow*

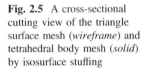

Fig. 2.5 A cross-sectional
cutting view of the triangle
surface mesh (*wireframe*) and
tetrahedral body mesh (*solid*)
by isosurface stuffing

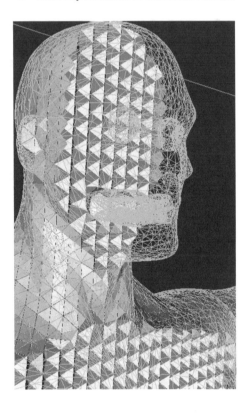

Some cases admit more than one possible stencil because the isosurface trun-
cates some BCC grid triangles, creating quadrilateral faces, each of which we bisect
into two triangles. Each stencil's tetrahedra are determined by the choice of diagonal used to bisect each quadrilateral. To choose diagonals, we use two disam-
biguation rules, designed to produce high-quality output tetrahedra.

Figure 2.5 shows a rendering result of the isosurface stuffing algorithms for a
human body.

2.3 Graded Interior Tetrahedra

This section addresses the need for a graded mesh that has uniformly fine elements
on its boundary, where accuracy is most crucial, but increasingly coarse elements
deeper into its interior. By reducing the number of tetrahedral in the mesh, we
reduce the FEM computation time.

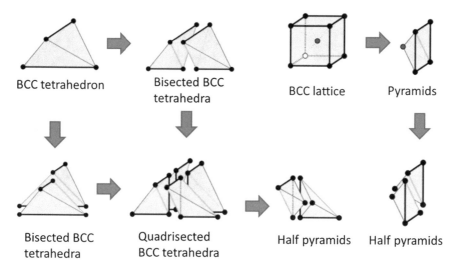

Fig. 2.6 Four categories of graded background grids: BCC tetrahedra, bisected BCC tetrahedra, quadrisected BCC tetrahedra, and half-pyramids

We replace the BCC grid with a graded background grid composed of four kinds of tetrahedra, as illustrated in Fig. 2.6. In addition to the BCC tetrahedron, we use a bisected BCC tetrahedron, created by splitting a BCC tetrahedron at the midpoint of one of its long edges, and a quadrisected BCC tetrahedron, created by splitting a bisected BCC tetrahedron along the surviving long edge. These tetrahedra are nearly as well shaped as the BCC tetrahedron. The fourth kind of tetrahedron is a half-pyramid. A cube can be divided into six pyramids, one for each face of the cube, with their apices meeting at the center of the cube, as illustrated. Each pyramid can be bisected by a diagonal into two half-pyramids. Half-pyramids can also be obtained by bisecting the red edge of a quadrisected BCC tetrahedron.

In addition to the black and red edges of the BCC grid, bisection and quadrisection also introduce a new kind of diagonal edge we call *blue edges*. Bisection and quadrisection also split black edges into shorter black edges, and quadrisection creates a new black edge which is axis-aligned.

We use an octree to help create a graded tetrahedral background grid using these four kinds of tetrahedra. The vertices of the background grid will be corners and centers of the octants (cubes) in the octree. As in the BCC grid, one tetrahedron can span two octants. If the octree were refined to the same depth everywhere, the background grid would be composed of BCC tetrahedra, except at its boundary. However, we try to refine the octree as little as possible, to minimize the number of tetrahedra.

Figure 2.7 shows the rendering result of the same human body with the graded background grid.

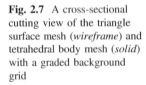

Fig. 2.7 A cross-sectional cutting view of the triangle surface mesh (*wireframe*) and tetrahedral body mesh (*solid*) with a graded background grid

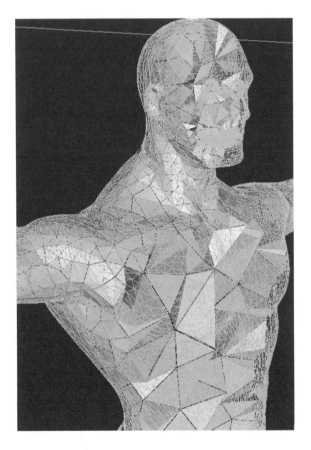

2.4 Summary

We have described a mesh generation algorithm, with simplicity and raw speed, for complicated shapes. Its attributes of speed, guaranteed quality, and numerical robustness make the isosurface stuffing algorithm suitable for robust remeshing in physically-based animation at interactive rates. The shortcomings of isosurface stuffing are its tendency to round off sharp corners and edges, and the reduction of guaranteed quality if the surface tetrahedra are not of uniform size.

Notes: Materials of this section are largely based on F. Labelle and J.R. Shewchuk's paper [1].

Reference

1. Labelle, F., Shewchuk, JR. FEM simulation of 3D deformable solids: A practitioner's guide to theory, discretization and model reduction. In *ACM SIGGRAPH 2007*.

Chapter 3
Dynamics Simulation in a Nutshell

Abstract In this chapter, we provide fundamental theories on continuum-based deformable models, including elasticity theory, finite element discretization, dynamics equations of motion and numerical integration schemes.

3.1 Introduction

Physically-based simulation of deformable models is based on continuum mechanics, and the mathematical models originated from engineering disciplines rather than computer science. Therefore, knowledge of fundamentals such as solid mechanics, elasticity theory, dynamics and numerical methods is a prerequisite for research on physics simulation.

In this chapter, we briefly introduce some of the essential concepts and for-mulations, which mainly include the following aspects:

- Important concepts in **solid mechanics**: strain, stress, elasticity, constitutive models, deformation energy, internal forces, etc.;
- The **finite element analysis/method**: as a numerical technique to solve continuum-based problems, by discretizing a continuous domain into small *finite elements*;
- **Time integration schemes**: numerical methods used to solve the dynamics equations of motion (i.e., system of differential equations with boundary value problems).

3.2 Elasticity in Three Dimensions

In three-dimensional space, deformation of a solid body can be formulated as a function $\phi : \mathbb{R}^3 \to \mathbb{R}^3$, mapping an *initial* (or *reference*) *configuration* into a *deformed configuration*. As shown in Fig. 3.1, a particle (*material point*) in the

J. Cai et al., *Graphical Simulation of Deformable Models*,
DOI 10.1007/978-3-319-51031-6_3

Fig. 3.1 Deformation mapping ϕ

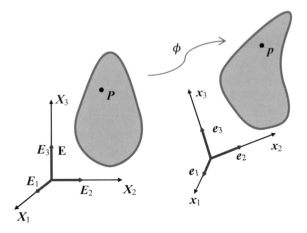

undeformed shape is denoted by the coordinate $X = (X_1, X_2, X_3) \in \mathbb{R}^3$ with respect to the Cartesian basis E_i, $i = 1, 2, 3$; the corresponding particle in the deformed shape is denoted as $x = (x_1, x_2, x_3) \in \mathbb{R}^3$ with respect to another Cartesian basis e_i. Generally, these two coordinate systems are coincident.

Thus we have the deformation mapping function as

$$x = \phi(X) \tag{3.1}$$

In dynamics simulation, this mapping also includes another *time* variable t as

$$x(t) = \phi(X, t)$$

This deformation can also be depicted by a *displacement* vector $u(X)$, such that

$$x = X + u(X). \tag{3.2}$$

3.2.1 Deformation Gradient

A key quantity in deformation analysis is the *deformation gradient*, defined as

$$F = \frac{\partial \phi(X)}{\partial X} = \frac{\partial x}{\partial X} = \frac{\partial u}{\partial X} + I, \tag{3.3}$$

where $I \in \mathbb{R}^{3 \times 3}$ is an identity matrix. From Eq. 3.3 we know that $F \in \mathbb{R}^{3 \times 3}$ is a second-order tensor,

$$F = \begin{pmatrix} \partial x_1/\partial X_1 & \partial x_1/\partial X_2 & \partial x_1/\partial X_3 \\ \partial x_2/\partial X_1 & \partial x_2/\partial X_2 & \partial x_2/\partial X_3 \\ \partial x_3/\partial X_1 & \partial x_3/\partial X_2 & \partial x_3/\partial X_3 \end{pmatrix}.$$

Meanings of F

The deformation gradient has certain physical meanings and contains the information connecting the initial and deformed configurations. For example, suppose that a material vector dX is deformed into a corresponding spatial vector dx, we have

$$dx = FdX.$$

Considering an element of infinitesimal volume in the original configuration, which is formed by three orthogonal material vectors $dX_i = dX_i E_i, i = 1, 2, 3$, the volume in the initial configuration can be computed as

$$dV = dX_1 \cdot dX_2 \times dX_3 = dX_1 dX_2 dX_3.$$

And the corresponding deformed volume dv is computed as

$$dv = (FdX_1) \cdot (FdX_2) \times (FdX_3) = \det(F) \, dV.$$

Therefore, the Jacobian $J = \det(F) = \frac{dv}{dV}$ represents the *fraction of volume change* during deformation.

Moreover, the deformation gradient can be decomposed by *polar decomposition* [1] into a *rotation tensor R* and a *stretch tensor U* as $F = RU$. So we get

$$dx = RUdX = R(UdX).$$

From this decomposition, it means that a material vector dX is firstly stretched in the material space, and then is rotated in the spatial space.

Notes and Remarks

From the value of J, we can judge how the volume changes during deformation. For example, $J = 1$ means no volume change; $J < 0$ means that there is inverted deformation. The invertible FEM model in [2] utilized the value to detect and deal with the issue of inverted elements.

In [3], the polar decomposition of F was used to construct a *rotation-strain space* that describes a deformed object with *rotation-strain coordinates*. As a descriptor of deformation, the *rotation-strain coordinates* were also exploited in shape interpolation and shape editing (e.g., [4]).

The deformation gradient F can be used as *measure* of deformation; however, due to its variance under rotations, it is not a proper choice. A better choice for the measure of deformation is described below.

3.2.2 *Deformation Measure by Strain Tensor*

3.2.2.1 The Nonlinear Green Strain Tensor

Given two material vectors dX_1, dX_2 in the reference configuration and their counterparts dx_1, dx_2 in the deformed configuration, a deformation can be measured by the difference of two scalar products, as

$$\frac{1}{2}(dx_1 \cdot dx_2 - dX_1 \cdot dX_2)$$
$$= \frac{1}{2}[(FdX_1) \cdot (FdX_2) - dX_1 \cdot dX_2]$$
$$= dX_1 \cdot \frac{1}{2}(F^T F - I)dX_2.$$

From the above, the right *Cauchy-Green deformation tensor* is defined, as

$$C = F^T F \in \mathbb{R}^{3 \times 3}. \tag{3.4}$$

and the *Green strain tensor* is defined as

$$\mathrm{E} = \frac{1}{2}(F^T F - I) \in \mathbb{R}^{3 \times 3}. \tag{3.5}$$

Thus we have

$$E = E(F) = \frac{1}{2}(C - I) = \frac{1}{2}\left[(RU)^T (RU) - I\right]$$
$$= \frac{1}{2}(U^2 - I) \tag{3.6}$$

It shows that the Green strain tensor $E \in \mathbb{R}^{3 \times 3}$ is symmetric, and *rotation invariant* by removing the effect of rotational transformation, with only deformation information contained in the quantity U^2. If a deformation only contains a pure rotation, i.e., $F = R$, then $E = \frac{1}{2}(R^T R - I) = 0$, meaning there is no deformation but a rigid transformation. With this rigid motion invariant property, F is often used as a *measure* of deformation in the literature. In the example-based method of [5], the Green strain tensor is used as a unique *descriptor* of element deformation.

From Eq. (3.6), we know that the Green strain tensor is *nonlinear* in terms of deformation (i.e., the displacement vector). Nonlinear elastic model based on this strain tensor is computationally expensive. In order to reduce computation and improve computational efficiency, a linearized strain tensor is often used in the case of small deformations as described below.

3.2.2.2 The Linear Cauchy Strain Tensor

The nonlinear Green strain can be linearized by *Taylor expansion* around the undeformed configuration (i.e., $F = I$) [6] to obtain a linearized form as

$$\varepsilon = \frac{1}{2}\left(F + F^T\right) - I = \frac{\partial \boldsymbol{u}}{\partial \boldsymbol{X}} + \left(\frac{\partial \boldsymbol{u}}{\partial \boldsymbol{X}}\right)^T \in \mathbb{R}^{3 \times 3}, \tag{3.7}$$

which is called the *Cauchy strain tensor* or the *small strain tensor*.

Since $\frac{\partial \boldsymbol{u}}{\partial \boldsymbol{X}} = \begin{pmatrix} \frac{\partial u}{\partial x} & \frac{\partial u}{\partial y} & \frac{\partial u}{\partial z} \\ \frac{\partial v}{\partial x} & \frac{\partial v}{\partial y} & \frac{\partial v}{\partial z} \\ \frac{\partial w}{\partial x} & \frac{\partial w}{\partial y} & \frac{\partial w}{\partial z} \end{pmatrix}$, we have

$$\begin{aligned} \varepsilon_{mat} :&= \begin{pmatrix} \varepsilon_{11} & \varepsilon_{12} & \varepsilon_{31} \\ \varepsilon_{21} & \varepsilon_{22} & \varepsilon_{23} \\ \varepsilon_{31} & \varepsilon_{32} & \varepsilon_{33} \end{pmatrix} \\ &= \begin{pmatrix} \frac{\partial u}{\partial x} & \frac{1}{2}\left(\frac{\partial u}{\partial y} + \frac{\partial v}{\partial x}\right) & \frac{1}{2}\left(\frac{\partial u}{\partial z} + \frac{\partial w}{\partial x}\right) \\ \frac{1}{2}\left(\frac{\partial v}{\partial x} + \frac{\partial u}{\partial y}\right) & \frac{\partial v}{\partial y} & \frac{1}{2}\left(\frac{\partial v}{\partial z} + \frac{\partial w}{\partial y}\right) \\ \frac{1}{2}\left(\frac{\partial w}{\partial x} + \frac{\partial u}{\partial z}\right) & \frac{1}{2}\left(\frac{\partial w}{\partial y} + \frac{\partial v}{\partial z}\right) & \frac{\partial w}{\partial z} \end{pmatrix}. \end{aligned}$$

Thus $\varepsilon_{mat} \in \mathbb{R}^{3 \times 3}$ is symmetric.

The advantage of using this linear strain tensor is that it greatly reduces computational complexity. However, it is not rotation invariant, thus is only suitable for small deformations [7].

3.2.3 Elasticity and Measure of Deformation Energy

Here we introduce *elasticity theory* from an energy perspective. Potential energy is stored in a deformed body, which is called the *strain energy*. If the strain energy only depends on the final deformed configuration and is independent of deformation paths, this kind of ideal elastic materials is considered being hyperelastic. For hyperelastic materials, the *strain-stress* relationship derives from a strain energy density function. Only *hyperelasticity* is discussed in our work, where an object is deformed under loads and returns to its original configuration when unloaded.

3.2.3.1 Constitutive Models of Isotropic Materials

In order to obtain the strain energy of a deformed body, a *strain-energy density* function $\psi(\phi; X)$ needs to defined, measuring the strain energy *per unit undeformed volume dV.* By integrating the energy density function over the entire undeformed domain Ω, we obtain the strain energy, as

$$W = \int_{\Omega} \psi(\phi; X) dV.$$

The strain-energy density function $\psi(\phi; X)$ can be defined by different mathematical models, which are called the **constitutive models**. A constitutive model connects the measure of deformation with the properties of a material.

A commonly used strain-energy density function for *isotropic* materials is defined as

$$\psi(\varepsilon) = \mu\varepsilon : \varepsilon + \frac{\lambda}{2}[tr(\varepsilon)]^2. \tag{3.8}$$

Here, $\varepsilon \in \mathbb{R}^{3\times 3}$ denotes a strain tensor [either in Eq. (3.5) or in Eq. (3.7)]. λ and μ are *Lamé coefficients*, which are related to *Young's modulus k* (as a measure of resistance of stretching) and *Poisson's ratio v* (as a measure of resistance of compression), and

$$\mu = \frac{\kappa}{2(1+v)}, \lambda = \frac{\kappa v}{(1+v)(1-2v)}.$$

If the nonlinear Green strain tensor E in Eq. (3.7) is used in place of ε, we get a simple *hyperelastic model* called *St. Venant-Kirchhoff* (StvK) model, which is often used in graphics community (e.g., [8]). There are many other constitutive models of isotropic materials, such as the *Mooney–Rivlin materials* and the *Neo-Hookean materials*, which are defines in terms of the invariants of the Cauchy-Green tensor in Eq. (3.4).

Notes and Remarks
In graphics applications, extremely large deformations and degenerate meshes often occur. These cause numerical instability of computation with the rigorously defined constitutive models. One possible solution is to modify a constitutive model (i.e., the deformation energy function) so that these extreme cases can be properly handled without affecting the normal deformation behaviors, such as [2, 9, 10] discussed in Sect. 1.3.1.2.

3.2.4 *Measure of Forces by Stress Tensor*

Another important quantity in solid mechanics is the *stress tensor*, which is a fundamental *force descriptor* that measures the internal forces incurred by deformation. The well-known *Cauchy stress tensor* σ is often used, measuring *force per unit area* in the current configuration. For a linear model, it can be computed as $\sigma = \frac{\partial \psi}{\partial \varepsilon}$.

In a contracted form, the symmetric strain tensor ε (either in Eq. 3.5), or in Eq. (3.7) can be written as a 6×1 vector as

$$
\begin{aligned}
\varepsilon &= \left(\varepsilon_{11}\ \varepsilon_{22}\ \varepsilon_{33}\ \gamma_{23}\ \gamma_{31}\ \gamma_{12}\right)^T \\
&= \left(\varepsilon_{11}\ \varepsilon_{22}\ \varepsilon_{33}\ 2\varepsilon_{23}\ 2\varepsilon_{31}\ 2\varepsilon_{12}\right)^T,
\end{aligned}
\tag{3.9}
$$

and then the contracted Cauchy stress vector is derived as

$$
\sigma = \left(\sigma_{11}, \sigma_{22}, \sigma_{33}, \sigma_{23}, \sigma_{31}, \sigma_{12}\right)^T = G\varepsilon,
$$

where G is called *material stiffness* matrix, as

$$
\begin{aligned}
G &= \begin{pmatrix}
2\mu + \lambda & \lambda & \lambda & 0 & 0 & 0 \\
\lambda & 2\mu + \lambda & \lambda & 0 & 0 & 0 \\
\lambda & \lambda & 2\mu + \lambda & 0 & 0 & 0 \\
0 & 0 & 0 & \mu & 0 & 0 \\
0 & 0 & 0 & 0 & \mu & 0 \\
0 & 0 & 0 & 0 & 0 & \mu
\end{pmatrix} \\
&= \frac{\kappa v}{(1+v)(1-2v)} \begin{pmatrix}
1-v & v & v & 0 & 0 & 0 \\
v & 1-v & v & 0 & 0 & 0 \\
v & v & 1-v & 0 & 0 & 0 \\
0 & 0 & 0 & \frac{1}{2}-v & 0 & 0 \\
0 & 0 & 0 & 0 & \frac{1}{2}-v & 0 \\
0 & 0 & 0 & 0 & 0 & \frac{1}{2}-v
\end{pmatrix}.
\end{aligned}
$$

Therefore, a *constitutive model* can also be defined in terms of stress-strain relationship.

Another two stress tensors commonly used are:

(1) The *First Piola–Kirchhoff stress tensor*, which can be interpreted as force (in the deformed configuration) per unit area (in the initial configuration),

$$
P = \frac{\partial \psi}{\partial F},
$$

which is used for computing internal forces in papers such as [2, 11, 12].

(2) The *Second Piola–Kirchhoff stress tensor*, which can be interpreted as force (in the initial configuration) per unit area (in the initial configuration) is defined as

$$S = \frac{\partial \psi}{\partial E} = 2 \frac{\partial \psi}{\partial C}.$$

The relationship between the two stress tensors is

$$P = FS.$$

3.3 Discretization with Finite Element Method

So far, all the physical quantities are described in a continuous space. However, in most cases it is difficult or impossible to find analytical solutions for a simulation problem with complex geometry. Therefore, it needs to be solved numerically. The most universal finite element formulation works on a large number of discretized elements. The discretization is established in the initial configuration using *isoparametric* elements ([13], Chaps. 16 and 18). The physical state (such as positions, displacements, and velocities) is assigned to the nodes of discretized mesh, and the continuous functions (such as deformation map, strain energy and internal forces) are reformulated in terms of the discrete variables.

In our work, we use a *tetrahedral mesh* as the representation of discretization, as shown in Fig. 3.2. Suppose that a tetrahedral mesh contains n nodes formed into n_e elements. For simplicity, we firstly discuss the related discretization within an element. The initial *nodal positions* of an element are defined as $\left(X_0^T, X_1^T, X_2^T, X_3^T\right)^T \in \mathbb{R}^{12 \times 1}$ where $X_i \in \mathbb{R}^{3 \times 1}$, $i = 1, \ldots, 4$, and the deformed counterpart as $\left(x_0^T, x_1^T, x_2^T, x_3^T\right)^T \in \mathbb{R}^{12 \times 1}$. By interpolation of geometry using standard shape functions $N_i(\xi) = N_i(\xi_1, \xi_2, \xi_3)$, a material point position in the initial configuration can be interpolated as $X = \sum_{i=1}^4 N_i(\xi)X_i$ and the deformed one as $x = \sum_{i=1}^4 N_i(\xi)x_i$. Thereafter, the following quantities can be computed:

(1) The **deformation gradient** is obtained by $F = \frac{\partial x}{\partial X} = \frac{\partial}{\partial X}\left(\sum_{i=1}^4 N_i(\xi)x_i\right)$, which involves solving the following term,

$$\frac{\partial N_i}{\partial X} = \left(\frac{\partial X}{\partial \xi}\right)^{-T} \frac{\partial N_i}{\partial \xi}.$$

(2) The **strain energy** is obtained by an integral of a given constitutive model $\psi(F)$,

$$W^e = \int_{\Omega^e} \psi(F)\, dV.$$

Fig. 3.2 A tetrahedral finite
element mesh

(3) The **nodal internal force** is computed as

$$f_i^e = -\frac{w^e}{x_i} \in \mathbb{R}^{3\times 1}, \quad i = 1,\ldots,4.$$

(4) The **element stiffness matrix** is computed as

$$K^e = \frac{\partial\left(f_1^e, f_2^e, f_3^e, f_4^e\right)}{\partial(x_1, x_2, x_3, x_4)} \in \mathbb{R}^{12\times 12}.$$

Assembly of all the elements can obtain the global internal force $f \in \mathbb{R}^{3n\times 1}$ and global stiffness matrix $K \in \mathbb{R}^{3n\times 3n}$.

3.4   Formulation of Dynamics Simulation

3.4.1   The Euler-Lagrangian Equations of Motion

Dynamics of a deformable object is governed by the *Euler-Lagrange equations* of motion, which are derived by Lagrangian mechanics [14, 15], as

$$M\ddot{u} + D\dot{u} + f_{int}(u) = f_{ext}$$
$$\text{or, } M\ddot{x} + D\dot{x} + f_{int}(x) = f_{ext} \tag{3.10}$$

where $u = u(t) \in \mathbb{R}^{3n \times 1}$ is the unknown displacement vector, $x = x(t) \in \mathbb{R}^{3n \times 1}$ the current positions vector, $M \in \mathbb{R}^{3n \times 3n}$ the mass matrix, $D\dot{u} \in \mathbb{R}^{3n}$ is the damping forces with $D \in \mathbb{R}^{3n \times 3n}$ as the damping coefficients, $f_{int}(u) \in \mathbb{R}^{3n \times 1}$ the internal forces, and $f_{ext} \in \mathbb{R}^{3n \times 1}$ the external forces. Since $x = X + u$, we have $\dot{x} = \dot{u}$, and $\ddot{x} = \ddot{u}$, and the two equations above are equivalent.

By applying

$$\begin{cases} \dot{v} = \ddot{u} = M^{-1}f \\ \dot{x} = v \end{cases}$$

where f denotes the resultant force, the second-order order equation in Eq. 3.10 can be transformed into a couple of first-order differential equations [16], which can be solved by a integration scheme discussed below.

3.4.2   Time Integration Schemes

3.4.2.1   Explicit Euler Time Integration

The simplest time integration method is the *explicit Euler integration* (also known as *forward Euler method*), with the time-stepping rules as

$$\begin{cases} v_{t+1} = v_t + h\dot{v}_t \\ x_{t+1} = x_t + hv_t \end{cases}, \tag{3.11}$$

where h is the size of each time step, and $\dot{v}_t = M^{-1}(f_{ext} + f_{int}(x_t) - Dv_t)$.

This explicit integration scheme proceeds blindly into the future. With relatively large time steps, it would increase the system energy (i.e., *overshooting problem*) and finally cause an explosion/failure of simulation. Thus, the step size has to be sufficiently small to ensure numerical stability ([17], Chap. 4).

3.4.2.2   Improved Explicit Integrators

To improve the stability of the explicit Euler method, a revised *symplectic Euler scheme* [18] can be applied, with the time-stepping rules as

$$\begin{cases} v_{t+1} = v_t + h\dot{v}_t \\ x_{t+1} = x_t + hv_{t+1} \end{cases}. \tag{3.12}$$

There are also other more accurate and stable schemes with higher degree of approximation, such as second and fourth order *Runge-Kutta* integrators, and *Verlet* integration (refer to [19] for more details).

3.4.2.3 Implicit Integration Method

A popular implicit integration scheme is the *implicit Euler method* (also known as *backward Euler method*) with time-stepping rules as follows

$$\begin{cases} v_{t+1} = v_t + h\dot{v}_{t+1} \\ x_{t+1} = x_t + hv_{t+1} \end{cases} \tag{3.13}$$

where $\dot{v}_{t+1} = M^{-1}(f_{ext} + f_{int}(x_{t+1}) - Dv_{t+1})$.

Other commonly used implicit schemes are the *Newmark* method and its variants [20], which have better energy conservation property. The implicit schemes are unconditionally stable. They lead to a large nonlinear system that is solved by *Newton's method* or some variation of Newton's method, which iteratively solves a large linear system of equations at each time step. Thus, it is much more computationally expensive than the explicit methods. Another issue is that it introduces numerical damping (i.e., energy dissipation) that dissipates energy (especially for the *backward Euler method*).

3.4.3 Variational/Optimization Implicit Euler

Another successful way of solving the dynamics problem is to recast the implicit integration of dynamics equations into a variational form, such that the time integration is as reformulated as an optimization problem.

For example, the system of differential equations in Eq. (3.13) are re-written as

$$M(x_{t+1} - x_t - hv_t) = h^2(f_{ext} + f_{int}(x_{t+1})), \tag{3.14}$$

where the damping term is omitted for brevity here. This system can be re-formulated to an optimization problem

$$min_{x_{t+1}} \left\{ \frac{1}{2h^2} \left\| M^{\frac{1}{2}}(x_{t+1} - s_n) \right\|_F^2 + W(x_{t+1}) \right\}, \tag{3.15}$$

where $s_n = x_{t+1} + hv_t + h^2 M^{-1} f_{ext}$, and $\|\cdot\|_F$ denotes the Frobenius norm, W is the strain energy.

For an optimization problem, more robust optimization strategies [21] can be employed, which can be more efficient than the nonlinear root-finding problem.

3.5 Summary

Physics simulation in computer graphics is a challenging task, which requires an integrated solution of linear algebra, differential equations, variational calculus (e.g., to understand the *Laplacian mechanics*), differential geometry, numerical methods, optimization, continuum mechanics, dynamics, etc.

We address the important concepts in solid mechanics. First, we give a brief introduction of continuum mechanics in combination with the finite element methods, dynamics equations and numerical integrations, which form an essential basis for our further research. Constitutive models are formulated for isotropic materials. Based on these foundations, we can investigate more complex aniso-tropic material models and their formulations, as presented in our work of Chaps. 4, 5, and 6.

Resorting to but not being strictly restricted by these physics principles, we also study geometrical techniques developed in computer graphics field, and combine them together to be better applied in graphics applications. With that, a physically based skeletal animation system is developed in Chap. 6.

References

1. Bonet, J., & Wood, R. D. (2008). *Nonlinear continuum mechanics for finite element analysis* (2nd ed.). Cambridge: Cambridge university press.
2. Irving, G., Teran, J., & Fedkiw, R. (2004). Invertible finite elements for robust simulation of large deformation. In *Proceedings of the 2004 ACM SIGGRAPH/Eurographics symposium on computer animation* (pp. 131–140). Grenoble, France: Eurographics Association.
3. Huang, J., et al. (2011). Interactive shape interpolation through controllable dynamic deformation. *IEEE Transactions on Visualization and Computer Graphics, 17*(7), 983–992.
4. Barbič, J., Sin, F., & Grinspun, E. (2012). Interactive editing of deformable simulations. ACM Transactions on Graphics (SIGGRAPH 2012), *31*(4).
5. Martin, S., et al. (2011). Example-based elastic materials. *ACM Transactions on Graphics (TOG), 30*(4), 72.
6. Fackler, P. L. (2005). Notes on matrix calculus. North Carolina State University.
7. Müller, M., & Gross, M. (2004). Interactive virtual materials. In *Proceedings of graphics interface* (pp. 239–246). London, Ontario, Canada: Canadian Human-Computer Communications Society.
8. Barbič, J., & James, D. L. (2005). Real-time subspace integration for St. Venant-Kirchhoff deformable models. In *ACM SIGGRAPH 2005 Papers* (pp. 982–990). Los Angeles, California: ACM.

9. Irving, G., Teran, J., & Fedkiw, R. (2006). Tetrahedral and hexahedral invertible finite elements. *Graphical Models, 68*(2), 66–89.
10. Stomakhin, A., et al. (2012). Energetically consistent invertible elasticity. In *Eurographics/ ACM SIGGRAPH symposium on computer animation*. The Eurographics Association.
11. Teran, J., et al. (2003). Finite volume methods for the simulation of skeletal muscle. In *Proceedings of the 2003 ACM SIGGRAPH/Eurographics symposium on computer animation* (pp. 68–74). San Diego, California: Eurographics Association.
12. An, S. S., Kim, T., & James, D. L. (2008). Optimizing cubature for efficient integration of subspace deformations. In *ACM Transactions on Graphics (TOG)*. New York: ACM.
13. Felippa, C. A. (2004) *Introduction to finite element methods*. Boulder: University of Colorado, http://www.colorado.edu/engineering/cas/courses.d/IFEM.d/
14. Morin, D. (2008). *Introduction to classical mechanics: with problems and solutions*. Cambridge: Cambridge University Press.
15. Shabana, A. A. (2009). *Computational dynamics*. Hoboken: Wiley.
16. Abell, M. L., & Braselton, J. P. (2014). Introductory differential equations: With boundary value problems. Amsterdam: Elsevier.
17. Fasshauer, G. (2007). Course notes: Numerical methods for differential equations/ computational mathematics II. http://www.math.iit.edu/~fass/478_578_handouts.html
18. Stern, A., & Desbrun, M. (2006). Discrete geometric mechanics for variational time integrators. In *ACM SIGGRAPH 2006 Courses*. New York: ACM.
19. Müller, M., et al. (2008). Real time physics: Class notes. In *ACM SIGGRAPH 2008 classes* (pp. 1–90). Los Angeles, California: ACM.
20. Wood, W. (1990). *Practical time-stepping schemes* (Vol. 6). Oxford, UK: Clarendon Press.
21. Nocedal, J., & Wright, S. (2006). *Numerical optimization*. Berlin: Springer Science & Business Media.

Chapter 4
Fiber Controls in FEM Model
for Transversely Isotropic Materials

Abstract In this chapter, we investigate transversely isotropic materials for the simulation of deformable objects with fibrous structures. In previous work, direction-dependent behaviors of transversely isotropic materials can only be achieved with an additional energy function which incorporates the material preferred direction. Such an additional energy term increases the computational complexity. We introduce a *fiber-field incorporated corotational finite element model* (CLFEM) that works directly with a constitutive model of transversely isotropic material. A smooth *fiber-field* is used to establish the local frames for each element. The orientation information of each element is incorporated into the CLFEM model by adding local transformations onto each element of the stiffness matrix.

4.1 Introduction

In this chapter, we investigate the modeling of *transversely isotropic* materials. Transversely isotropic materials have symmetric mechanical properties about an axis that is normal to a plane of isotropy. They are commonly found in real-world objects with fibrous structures, such as plants and biological soft tissues. Simulating these deformable objects using transversely isotropic materials can generate more realistic behaviors than using isotropic ones.

In virtual surgery applications, transversely isotropic materials are often used for modeling soft tissues [1]. Picinbono et al. [2] presented a linear elasticity model combined with a fiber-reinforced energy, and later they proposed a nonlinear elasticity model to better support large deformations [3]. Irving et al. [4] proposed an invertible FEM model to deal with degenerate and inverted elements during large deformations, which is applicable to transversely isotropic materials. Teran et al. [5] proposed to use *B-spline solids* for assigning fiber directions to each element of a simulated mesh, and a *finite volume method* was used to simulate muscles. In [6], a fiber-reinforced model was presented that some curves (as the fibers) are interactively embedded into a solid object, and the internal forces are

© Springer International Publishing Switzerland 2016
J. Cai et al., *Graphical Simulation of Deformable Models*,
DOI 10.1007/978-3-319-51031-6_4

then computed in terms of deformation energies of both the isotropic solid and the curves.

In previous works, directional dependent behaviors of transversely isotropic material are achieved by introducing an additional energy incorporating material preferred directions. The total deformation energy is the sum of an *isotropic* strain energy and a fiber-reinforced strain energy. This kind of approaches can produce physically-plausible results, but the additional energy term increases computational cost. Here we present a fiber-field incorporated corotational FEM model that works directly with the constitutive model of transversely isotropic materials. Furthermore, a smooth *fiber-field* is used to establish local frames for each element, which is used as references for defining material properties. This orientation information of each element is incorporated into the corotational FEM model, through adding a local transformation upon each elemental stiffness matrix.

Large deformations are supported, and physically-realistic deformations can be achieved. With pre-computation, it adds no computational cost on the existing corotational FEM model during simulation. Meanwhile, it provides a directable control of anisotropic behaviors, which is desirable for designing anisotropic deformable models.

4.2 Constitutive Model of Transversely Isotropic Materials

Let's start with the measure of deformation. For a solid object, the deformation gradient is defined as $= \frac{\partial x}{\partial X} \in \mathbb{R}^{3\times3}$, where $X \in \mathbb{R}^3$ denotes the undeformed material point in the material space and $x \in \mathbb{R}^3$ is the corresponding deformed point. The *small strain tensor* $\varepsilon = (F^T + F)/2 - I$ is used in our work for its computational efficiency (refer to Sect. 3.2.2).

In continuum mechanics, mechanical behaviors of a material are defined by a *constitutive model* (refer to Sect. 3.2.3), which represents the relationship between stress and strain as $\sigma = C\varepsilon$, where σ and ε are second-order stress and strain tensor respectively, C is a fourth-order tensor called *elastic stiffness* [7]. Due to the symmetry property of the strain tensor, the relationship can be written in a contracted form as

$$
\begin{Bmatrix} \sigma_{11} \\ \sigma_{22} \\ \sigma_{33} \\ \sigma_{23} \\ \sigma_{31} \\ \sigma_{12} \end{Bmatrix} = \begin{pmatrix} C_{11} & C_{12} & C_{13} & 0 & 0 & 0 \\ & C_{22} & C_{23} & 0 & 0 & 0 \\ & & C_{33} & 0 & 0 & 0 \\ & & & C_{44} & 0 & 0 \\ & sym. & & & C_{55} & 0 \\ & & & & & C_{66} \end{pmatrix} \begin{Bmatrix} \varepsilon_{11} \\ \varepsilon_{22} \\ \varepsilon_{33} \\ 2\varepsilon_{23} \\ 2\varepsilon_{31} \\ 2\varepsilon_{12} \end{Bmatrix}, \quad (4.1)
$$

where it has

$$C_{11} = C_{22}, \; C_{13} = C_{23}, \; C_{55} = C_{66}, \; C_{44} = \frac{1}{2}(C_{11} - C_{12}),$$

with the third material axis as the axis of symmetry. Thus, there are totally *five* independent material parameters for a transversely isotropic material.

4.3   Fiber-Field Incorporated FEM Model

In order to simulate a deformable model with transversely isotropic materials, we propose to incorporate a *fiber-field* that contains material orientation information into the corotational linear FEM (CLFEM) model [8]. Large deformations are allowed without visual artifact of distorted volumes.

Firstly a brief formulation of the CLFEM model is described. Then we explain how to incorporate the fiber orientation information with CLFEM. Finally we present the formulation for dynamics simulation using implicit time integration. Note that for clarity most of the formulations here are based on a single tetrahedral (TET) element, where the symbols of mechanical quantities are denoted with a superscript 'e'. A tetrahedral element is denoted by its nodal positions $X^e = (X_0^T, X_1^T, X_2^T, X_3^T)^T \in \mathbb{R}^{12 \times 1}$ where $X_i \in \mathbb{R}^{3 \times 1}$ in the initial configuration, and $x^e = (x_0^T, x_1^T, x_2^T, x_3^T)^T \in \mathbb{R}^{12 \times 1}$ as a counterpart in the deformed configuration.

4.3.1   The CLFEM Model

The linear FEM model is only suitable for infinitesimal deformations (refer to Sect. 3.2.2.2), and obvious volume distortion artifact occurs when an object is under large deformations (as shown in Fig. 4.7b). The CLFEM model improves the linear FEM model by removing the rotational effect of deformations. As shown in Fig. 4.1, $R \in \mathbb{R}^{3 \times 3}$ is a rotational transformation from the initial configuration to the deformed shape, then the elemental internal forces $f_{int}^e \in \mathbb{R}^{12 \times 1}$ are computed as

$$f_{int}^e = \begin{pmatrix} R & 0 & 0 & 0 \\ 0 & R & 0 & 0 \\ 0 & 0 & R & 0 \\ 0 & 0 & 0 & R \end{pmatrix} K^e \left(\begin{bmatrix} R^T x_0 \\ R^T x_1 \\ R^T x_2 \\ R^T x_3 \end{bmatrix} - \begin{bmatrix} X_0 \\ X_1 \\ X_2 \\ X_3 \end{bmatrix} \right) = R^e K^e \left(R^{e^T} x^e - X^e \right), \quad (4.2)$$

where $R^e \in \mathbb{R}^{12 \times 12}$, and $K^e \in \mathbb{R}^{12 \times 12}$ is a constant element stiffness matrix.

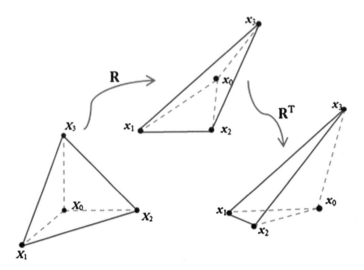

Fig. 4.1 The CLFEM model

4.3.2 Fiber-Field Incorporated FEM Model

Now we present the mechanism for a fiber-field incorporated FEM model. Each TET element is assign with a direction vector, which forms a volumetric fiber-field for the whole TET mesh. For deformable objects with internal fiber structures, it is these internal fiber structures that actually affect their transversely anisotropic behaviors. Based on this observation, we formulate an FEM model by utilizing orientation information of a fiber-field that is smoothly distributed inside an object.

Suppose a fiber-field, which consists of a preferred direction for each element, is given. An example is shown in Fig. 4.3c. Then a local orthonormal frame $\{q_1, q_2, q_3\}$ where $q_i \in \mathbb{R}^{3 \times 1}$, is established for each element: with one axis in accordance with the fiber orientation (here we use q_3). Since material properties are symmetric about the q_3 axis, the orientations of q_1 and q_2 are arbitrary and are only required to be on the plane perpendicular to q_3. We define a local orientation matrix as $Q^e = (q_1, q_2, q_3) \in \mathbb{R}^{3 \times 3}$, and denote a quantity in this local frame by a hatted symbol $\widehat{}$, e.g., $\widehat{K^e}$ is denoted as a local element stiffness matrix. The matrix Q^e plays an essential role in our model, and it is extended to a 12×12 matrix like R^e and represented by a same notation for simplicity.

In our approach, instead of computing the element stiffness matrix in a global frame, which is the case for simulation of isotropic materials, we do computation in the local frames. The element internal forces and stiffness matrix are computed by the following procedure:

(1) Firstly, the displacement vector $\widehat{\boldsymbol{u}^e} \in \mathbb{R}^{12\times1}$ in the local frame of an element is computed as

$$\widehat{\boldsymbol{u}^e} = Q^{e^T}(R^{e^T}\boldsymbol{x}^e - \boldsymbol{X}^e).$$

where $R^e, Q^e \in \mathbb{R}^{12\times12}$.

(2) The local constant element stiffness matrix $\widehat{K^e}$ is computed as

$$\widehat{K^e} = \widehat{B}^T C \widehat{B}\, V^e,$$

where V^e is the volume of the element, and $\widehat{B} \in \mathbb{R}^{6\times12}$ is the *strain-displacement matrix* that is also computed locally in terms of $\widehat{\boldsymbol{u}^e}$.

(3) The local element internal forces are computed as

$$\widehat{\boldsymbol{f}^e}_{int} = \widehat{K^e}\widehat{\boldsymbol{u}^e}.$$

(4) Finally, the element internal forces in the global frame are obtained, as

$$\boldsymbol{f}^e_{int} = R^e Q^e \widehat{\boldsymbol{f}^e}_{int} = R^e Q^e \widehat{K^e} Q^{e^T}(R^{e^T}\boldsymbol{x}^e - \boldsymbol{X}^e) = R^e K^e \left(R^{e^T}\boldsymbol{x}^e - \boldsymbol{X}^e\right), \quad (4.3)$$

where $K^e = Q^e \widehat{K^e} Q^{e^T}$ is the new element stiffness matrix of our model.

By *assembly of elements*, the matrices K^e of all the elements can be assembled to a global stiffness matrix $\bar{K} \in \mathbb{R}^{3n\times3n}$, where n is the total number of elements. Due to the fact that Q^e is pre-defined which is unchanged during simulation, $\bar{K}$ can also be pre-computed. Therefore, in our fiber-field incorporated model, no additional computational cost is introduced to the original CLFEM simulation.

- **FEM Discretization: Stiffness Matrix Computation**

A tetrahedral element has undeformed position vector $(\boldsymbol{X}_0, \boldsymbol{X}_1, \boldsymbol{X}_2, \boldsymbol{X}_3) \in \mathbb{R}^{12\times1}$, and the displacement vector is $(\boldsymbol{u}_0, \boldsymbol{u}_1, \boldsymbol{u}_2, \boldsymbol{u}_3) \in \mathbb{R}^{12\times1}$.

Method1: By Strain-Displacement Matrix

1. Element Shape Functions Fig. 4.2

Natural shape functions $\{N_0, N_1, N_2, N_3\}$:

$$\begin{cases} N_0(\xi, \eta, \varphi) = \varsigma = 1 - \xi - \eta - \varphi \\ N_1(\xi, \eta, \varphi) = \xi \\ N_2(\xi, \eta, \varphi) = \eta \\ N_3(\xi, \eta, \varphi) = \varphi \end{cases}$$

And $0 \le N_i \le 1$, $\sum_{i=0}^{3} N_i = 1$

2. Geometric Interpolation

$$X = \begin{pmatrix} X \\ Y \\ Z \end{pmatrix} = \sum_{i=0}^{3} N_i X_i = \begin{pmatrix} N_0 & 0 & 0 & N_1 & 0 & 0 & N_2 & 0 & 0 & N_3 & 0 & 0 \\ 0 & N_0 & 0 & 0 & N_1 & 0 & 0 & N_2 & 0 & 0 & N_3 & 0 \\ 0 & 0 & N_0 & 0 & 0 & N_1 & 0 & 0 & N_2 & 0 & 0 & N_3 \end{pmatrix} \begin{pmatrix} X_0 \\ Y_0 \\ Z_0 \\ X_1 \\ Y_1 \\ Z_1 \\ X_2 \\ Y_2 \\ Z_2 \\ X_3 \\ Y_3 \\ Z_3 \end{pmatrix}$$

$$= \begin{pmatrix} u \\ v \\ w \end{pmatrix} = \sum_{i=0}^{3} N_i u_i$$

$$= \begin{pmatrix} N_0 & 0 & 0 & N_1 & 0 & 0 & N_2 & 0 & 0 & N_3 & 0 & 0 \\ 0 & N_0 & 0 & 0 & N_1 & 0 & 0 & N_2 & 0 & 0 & N_3 & 0 \\ 0 & 0 & N_0 & 0 & 0 & N_1 & 0 & 0 & N_2 & 0 & 0 & N_3 \end{pmatrix} \begin{pmatrix} u_0 \\ v_0 \\ w_0 \\ u_1 \\ v_1 \\ w_1 \\ u_2 \\ v_2 \\ w_2 \\ u_3 \\ v_3 \\ w_3 \end{pmatrix}$$

$$= Nd.$$

Finite elements constructed in this way are known as *isoparametric finite element*.

3. Linear Strain Vector

$$\varepsilon = \begin{pmatrix} \frac{\partial}{\partial X} & 0 & 0 \\ 0 & \frac{\partial}{\partial Y} & 0 \\ 0 & 0 & \frac{\partial}{\partial Z} \\ \frac{\partial}{\partial Y} & \frac{\partial}{\partial X} & 0 \\ 0 & \frac{\partial}{\partial Z} & \frac{\partial}{\partial Y} \\ \frac{\partial}{\partial Z} & 0 & \frac{\partial}{\partial X} \end{pmatrix} \begin{pmatrix} u \\ v \\ w \end{pmatrix} = Lu$$

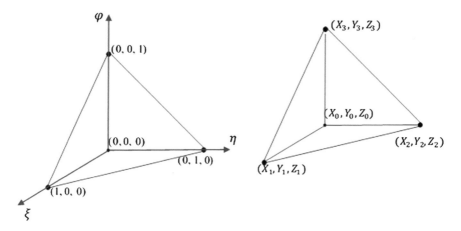

Fig. 4.2 Isoparametric mapping for a linear tetrahedral element

$$\varepsilon = LN\boldsymbol{d} = B\boldsymbol{d}$$

L: strain operator
B: strain-displacement matrix

4. Computation of Strain-Displacement Matrix $\boldsymbol{B}$

$$B = \begin{pmatrix} \frac{\partial N_0}{\partial X} & 0 & 0 & \frac{\partial N_1}{\partial X} & 0 & 0 & \frac{\partial N_2}{\partial X} & 0 & 0 & \frac{\partial N_3}{\partial X} & 0 & 0 \\ 0 & \frac{\partial N_0}{\partial Y} & 0 & 0 & \frac{\partial N_1}{\partial Y} & 0 & 0 & \frac{\partial N_2}{\partial Y} & 0 & 0 & \frac{\partial N_3}{\partial Y} & 0 \\ 0 & 0 & \frac{\partial N_0}{\partial Z} & 0 & 0 & \frac{\partial N_1}{\partial Z} & 0 & 0 & \frac{\partial N_2}{\partial Z} & 0 & 0 & \frac{\partial N_3}{\partial Z} \\ \frac{\partial N_0}{\partial Y} & \frac{\partial N_0}{\partial X} & 0 & \frac{\partial N_1}{\partial Y} & \frac{\partial N_1}{\partial X} & 0 & \frac{\partial N_2}{\partial Y} & \frac{\partial N_2}{\partial X} & 0 & \frac{\partial N_3}{\partial Y} & \frac{\partial N_3}{\partial X} & 0 \\ 0 & \frac{\partial N_0}{\partial Z} & \frac{\partial N_0}{\partial Y} & 0 & \frac{\partial N_1}{\partial Z} & \frac{\partial N_1}{\partial Y} & 0 & \frac{\partial N_2}{\partial Z} & \frac{\partial N_2}{\partial Y} & 0 & \frac{\partial N_3}{\partial Z} & \frac{\partial N_3}{\partial Y} \\ \frac{\partial N_0}{\partial Z} & 0 & \frac{\partial N_0}{\partial X} & \frac{\partial N_1}{\partial Z} & 0 & \frac{\partial N_1}{\partial X} & \frac{\partial N_2}{\partial Z} & 0 & \frac{\partial N_2}{\partial X} & \frac{\partial N_3}{\partial Z} & 0 & \frac{\partial N_3}{\partial X} \end{pmatrix},$$

Thus we need to compute $\frac{\partial N_i}{\partial X}$, $\frac{\partial N_i}{\partial Y}$, *and* $\frac{\partial N_i}{\partial Z}$ Since that

$$\begin{pmatrix} \frac{\partial N_i}{\partial \xi} \\ \frac{\partial N_i}{\partial \eta} \\ \frac{\partial N_i}{\partial \varphi} \end{pmatrix} = \begin{pmatrix} \frac{dX}{d\xi} & \frac{dY}{d\xi} & \frac{dZ}{d\xi} \\ \frac{dX}{d\eta} & \frac{dY}{d\eta} & \frac{dZ}{d\eta} \\ \frac{dX}{d\varphi} & \frac{dY}{d\varphi} & \frac{dZ}{d\varphi} \end{pmatrix} \begin{pmatrix} \frac{\partial N_i}{\partial X} \\ \frac{\partial N_i}{\partial Y} \\ \frac{\partial N_i}{\partial Z} \end{pmatrix} = J \begin{pmatrix} \frac{\partial N_i}{\partial X} \\ \frac{\partial N_i}{\partial Y} \\ \frac{\partial N_i}{\partial Z} \end{pmatrix},$$

we have

$$
\begin{pmatrix} \frac{\partial N_i}{\partial X} \\ \frac{\partial N_i}{\partial Y} \\ \frac{\partial N_i}{\partial Z} \end{pmatrix} = J^{-1} \begin{pmatrix} \frac{\partial N_i}{\partial \xi} \\ \frac{\partial N_i}{\partial \eta} \\ \frac{\partial N_i}{\partial \varphi} \end{pmatrix}.
$$

Since that

$$
N_0 = \varsigma = 1 - \xi - \eta - \varphi \quad \rightarrow \quad \frac{\partial N_0}{\partial \xi} = -1, \quad \frac{\partial N_0}{\partial \eta} = -1, \quad \frac{\partial N_0}{\partial \varphi} = -1
$$

$$
N_1 = \xi \quad \rightarrow \quad \frac{\partial N_1}{\partial \xi} = 1, \quad \frac{\partial N_1}{\partial \eta} = 0, \quad \frac{\partial N_1}{\partial \varphi} = 0
$$

$$
N_2 = \eta \quad \rightarrow \quad \frac{\partial N_2}{\partial \xi} = 0, \quad \frac{\partial N_2}{\partial \eta} = 1, \quad \frac{\partial N_2}{\partial \varphi} = 0
$$

$$
N_3 = \varphi \quad \rightarrow \quad \frac{\partial N_3}{\partial \xi} = 0, \quad \frac{\partial N_3}{\partial \eta} = 0, \quad \frac{\partial N_3}{\partial \varphi} = 1
$$

We have

$$
J = \begin{pmatrix} \frac{dX}{d\xi} & \frac{dY}{d\xi} & \frac{dZ}{d\xi} \\ \frac{dX}{d\eta} & \frac{dY}{d\eta} & \frac{dZ}{d\eta} \\ \frac{dX}{d\varphi} & \frac{dY}{d\varphi} & \frac{dZ}{d\varphi} \end{pmatrix} = \begin{pmatrix} \frac{\partial N_0}{\partial \xi} & \frac{\partial N_1}{\partial \xi} & \frac{\partial N_2}{\partial \xi} & \frac{\partial N_3}{\partial \xi} \\ \frac{\partial N_0}{\partial \eta} & \frac{\partial N_1}{\partial \eta} & \frac{\partial N_2}{\partial \eta} & \frac{\partial N_3}{\partial \eta} \\ \frac{\partial N_0}{\partial \varphi} & \frac{\partial N_1}{\partial \varphi} & \frac{\partial N_2}{\partial \varphi} & \frac{\partial N_3}{\partial \varphi} \end{pmatrix} \begin{pmatrix} X_0 & Y_0 & Z_0 \\ X_1 & Y_1 & Z_1 \\ X_2 & Y_2 & Z_2 \\ X_3 & Y_3 & Z_3 \end{pmatrix}
$$

$$
= \begin{pmatrix} -1 & 1 & 0 & 0 \\ -1 & 0 & 1 & 0 \\ -1 & 0 & 0 & 1 \end{pmatrix} \begin{pmatrix} X_0 & Y_0 & Z_0 \\ X_1 & Y_1 & Z_1 \\ X_2 & Y_2 & Z_2 \\ X_3 & Y_3 & Z_3 \end{pmatrix} = \begin{pmatrix} X_1 - X_0 & Y_1 - Y_0 & Z_1 - Z_0 \\ X_2 - X_0 & Y_2 - Y_0 & Z_2 - Z_0 \\ X_3 - X_0 & Y_3 - Y_0 & Z_3 - Z_0 \end{pmatrix}.
$$

From the above we know that J is constant and thus B is constant. And we can obtain $\frac{\partial N_i}{\partial X}, \frac{\partial N_i}{\partial Y}, \text{ and } \frac{\partial N_i}{\partial Z}$ by

$$
\begin{pmatrix} \frac{\partial N_i}{\partial X} \\ \frac{\partial N_i}{\partial Y} \\ \frac{\partial N_i}{\partial Z} \end{pmatrix} = J^{-1} \begin{pmatrix} \frac{\partial N_i}{\partial \xi} \\ \frac{\partial N_i}{\partial \eta} \\ \frac{\partial N_i}{\partial \varphi} \end{pmatrix},
$$

For example,
$$
\begin{pmatrix} \frac{\partial N_0}{\partial X} \\ \frac{\partial N_0}{\partial Y} \\ \frac{\partial N_0}{\partial Z} \end{pmatrix} = J^{-1} \begin{pmatrix} -1 \\ -1 \\ -1 \end{pmatrix}.
$$

5. Internal Forces and Stiffness matrix

(1) Strain energy:

$$U = \int_\Omega \frac{1}{2}(Bd)^T G(Bd)\,d\Omega = \frac{1}{2}d^{\mathrm{T}} \int_\Omega B^T GB\,d\Omega\,d.$$

(2) Element internal force:

$$\mathbf{f}_{int} = \frac{\partial U}{\partial \mathbf{d}} = \int_\Omega B^T GB\,d\Omega\,\mathbf{d} = K^e \mathbf{d}.$$

(3) Element Stiffness Matrix:

$$K^e = \int_\Omega B^T GB\,d\Omega = V^e(B^T GB).$$

And the volume of undeformed element: $V^e = \frac{1}{6}(\mathbf{x}_1 - \mathbf{x}_0, \mathbf{x}_2 - \mathbf{x}_0, \mathbf{x}_3 - \mathbf{x}_0)$.

Method2: By Approximate Deformation Gradient

Deformed position vector $(\mathbf{x}_0, \mathbf{x}_1, \mathbf{x}_2, \mathbf{x}_3) \in \mathbb{R}^{12\times 1}$

1. Approximated deformation gradient

   Frome $d\mathbf{x} = Fd\mathbf{X}$, we have

$$\begin{pmatrix} x_1 - x_0 & x_2 - x_0 & x_3 - x_0 \\ y_1 - y_0 & y_2 - y_0 & y_3 - y_0 \\ z_1 - z_0 & z_2 - z_0 & z_3 - z_0 \end{pmatrix} = F \begin{pmatrix} X_1 - X_0 & X_2 - X_0 & X_3 - X_0 \\ Y_1 - Y_0 & Y_2 - Y_0 & Y_3 - Y_0 \\ Z_1 - Z_0 & Z_2 - Z_0 & Z_3 - Z_0 \end{pmatrix}.$$

   Thus we get

$$\begin{aligned} F &= \begin{pmatrix} x_1 - x_0 & x_2 - x_0 & x_3 - x_0 \\ y_1 - y_0 & y_2 - y_0 & y_3 - y_0 \\ z_1 - z_0 & z_2 - z_0 & z_3 - z_0 \end{pmatrix} \begin{pmatrix} X_1 - X_0 & X_2 - X_0 & X_3 - X_0 \\ Y_1 - Y_0 & Y_2 - Y_0 & Y_3 - Y_0 \\ Z_1 - Z_0 & Z_2 - Z_0 & Z_3 - Z_0 \end{pmatrix}^{-1} \\ &= D_s D_m^{-1}. \end{aligned}$$

1. Linear strain
   From $\varepsilon_{mat} := \frac{1}{2}(F + F^{\mathrm{T}}) - I$, we get the contracted form $\boldsymbol{\varepsilon}$.
2. Strain energy density

$$\psi(F) = \frac{1}{2}\varepsilon^T G\varepsilon$$

3. Strain energy

$$U = V^e \psi(F)$$

4. Internal force (on nodes) and stiffness matrix

$$f_{int} = \frac{\partial U}{\partial(X_0, X_1, X_2, X_3)} \in \mathbb{R}^{12 \times 1}$$

$$K^e = \frac{\partial f_{int}}{\partial(X_0, X_1, X_2, X_3)} \in \mathbb{R}^{12 \times 12}$$

Remarks Method 1 is more suitable for linear FEM, since the stiffness matrix is constant and independent of the deformed configuration, and thus can be pre-computed; Method 2 depends on the deformed configuration, thus the stiffness matrix cannot be precomputed, which is more suitable for nonlinear FEM, i.e., with the nonlinear Green tensor.

4.4 Implicit Time Integration for Dynamics

For the simulation of dynamic deformation, the dynamics equations of motion are then given by a system of second-order ordinary differential equations (refer to Sect. 3.4.1):

$$M\ddot{u} + D\dot{u} + f_{int} = f_{ext}$$

For a tetrahedral mesh with n vertices, $u \in \mathbb{R}^{3n \times 1}$, $\dot{u}$ and $\ddot{u}$ are velocity and acceleration vectors respectively. $M \in \mathbb{R}^{3n \times 3n}$ is the mass matrix, D the damping matrix, $f_{int} \in \mathbb{R}^{3n \times 1}$ the internal forces, and $f_{ext} \in \mathbb{R}^{3n \times 1}$ the applied external forces.

An *implicit backward Euler* integration scheme [9] is used in our model, for the reason that it is stable and suitable for large time steps. The time-stepping rules are as follows:

$$\begin{aligned} \dot{u}_{t+1} &= \dot{u}_t + h\ddot{u}_{t+1} \\ u_{t+1} &= u_t + h\dot{u}_{t+1} \end{aligned} \tag{4.4}$$

where h is the size of each time step. At time $(t+1)$, we get

$$\begin{aligned} \dot{u}_{t+1} &= \dot{u}_t + hM^{-1}\left[f_{ext} - D\dot{u}_{t+1} - R\bar{K}\left(R^T x_{t+1} - x_0\right)\right] \\ x_{t+1} &= x_t + h\dot{u}_{t+1} \end{aligned} \tag{4.5}$$

Finally we can get a linear system:

$$\left(M + hD + h^2 R\bar{K}R^T\right)\dot{u}_{t+1} = M\dot{u}_t + h\left(f_{ext} - R\bar{K}R^T x_t + R\bar{K}x_0\right) \tag{4.6}$$

By solving the linear system, the simulation state (velocity and position vectors) can be updated. Here, it shows the advantage of the CLFEM model that there is no need of re-computing the stiffness matrix at each step (unlike the nonlinear model, the tangent stiffness matrix has to be updated at each iteration in an iterative solver), but only to update the element rotation matrices.

4.5   Experiments and Assessments

To assess the effectiveness of our algorithm, in this section, we construct several dynamics simulations of deformable objects with transversely isotropic materials. Here, a tetrahedral mesh is used as a discretized representation of a solid body, with an embedded high resolution surface mesh for rendering purpose, as shown in Fig. 4.3a, the transparent mesh denotes a tetrahedral mesh, with a high resolution textured surface mesh embedded inside it. Note that the green dots represent nodes fixed in positions.

Without loss of generality, the fiber-field of a tetrahedral mesh is generated by a sketch-based interface (as in [10, 11]). The user is allowed to draw a few strokes on the surface or a sliced internal surface boundary of the tetrahedral mesh, to roughly define the fiber directions; as shown in Fig. 4.3b, the red lines are the strokes by the user. Then, a smooth interpolation is performed to automatically generate a smooth fiber orientation field on each nodes of the tetrahedral mesh. Eventually, a fiber orientation is generated for each tetrahedron element with *barycentric interpolation* of the orientations of its four nodes; as shown in Fig. 4.3c, the generated fiber-field vectors are rendered as purple line segments.

(a)   **(b)**   **(c)**

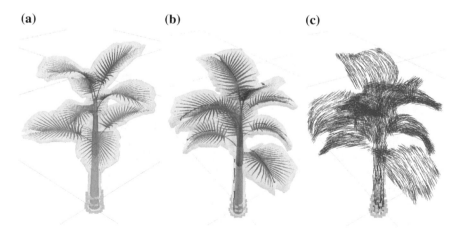

Fig. 4.3 a A palm tree model with a volumetric mesh and an embedded surface mesh; **b** user-defined strokes (*red*); **c** a fiber-field of all the tetrahedral elements

4.5.1 Impact of Fiber Field on the Elastic Stiffness

As in Eq. (4.1), five parameters, which represent the material's resistance to normal and shear deformations, can be used to define a transversely isotropic material. For comparison, we start with an isotropic material that has

$$C_{11} = C_{22} = C_{33} = \lambda + 2\mu, C_{12} = C_{13} = C_{23} = \lambda, C_{44} = C_{55} = C_{66} = \mu,$$

where λ and μ are *Lamé coefficients* (related to Young's modulus and Poisson's ratio). It can be changed according to Eq. (4.1) while keeping its positive-definiteness. Changing C_{33} to a larger value makes the material stiffer along the fiber orientation. Likewise, other parameters can also be changed to alter the material's resistance to normal and shear forces with respect to the local frame Q^e.

A comparison for a simple cubic model is shown in Fig. 4.4. Under gravity, the cubic model of isotropic material in Fig. 4.4c deforms uniformly, while the transversely isotropic model in Fig. 4.4d shows anisotropic behavior, which is in accordance with the fiber-field in Fig. 4.4b.

4.5.2 Fibers with Heterogeneous Materials

To demonstrate the capability of our fiber-field incorporated FEM model, a complex palm tree model made of heterogeneous materials is simulated, i.e., the trunk and leaves have different material properties. In Fig. 4.5, we show the deformations of the palm tree model under gravity. Figure 4.5a shows the original undeformed model. As a basis for comparisons, Fig. 4.5b shows deformation of the tree made of an isotropic material. Being physically-plausible, it bends to the ground if the material is too soft (or, inflexible to move if the material is too stiff). Figure 4.5c shows the tree consisting of heterogeneous materials: it has stronger support from its trunk, preventing unnatural bending, but it is very difficult to obtain physically-plausible behavior for the leaves by tuning isotropic parameters. In nature, a leaf is much stiffer along its vein than in the other directions, and the tree also exhibits a stiffer material property along its trunk. Based on this observation, we should use a transversely isotropic material with a larger value of C_{33}. By using the fiber-field incorporated FEM model, Fig. 4.5d shows a physically-plausible deformation of the palm tree: it becomes stiffer along the fibers while being flexible in the other directions. Figure 4.6 shows the comparison of deformations under gravity and a dragging force. In contrast to the unnatural deformations of an isotropic model in Fig. 4.6a, the fiber-field incorporated model in Fig. 4.6b exhibits strong stiffness along fiber directions that prevents over-bending of the trunk and over-stretching of the leaves.

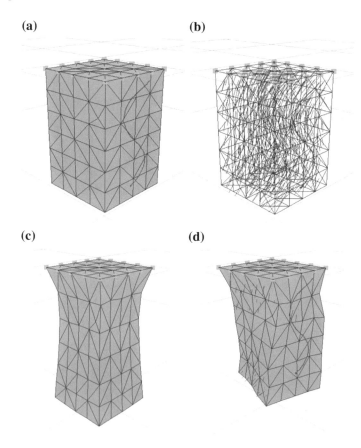

Fig. 4.4 Deformation of transversely isotropic material with a fiber-field **a** drawing strokes on undeformed model; **b** element fiber-field; **c** deformation under gravity (isotropic material); **d** deformation under gravity (transversely isotropic material)

Besides its convincing improvement in the visual results in physically-plausible deformation, the fiber-field incorporated FEM model only adds computational cost in the pre-computation step, thus achieving the same performance as the existing CLFEM model. In our experiments, both the palm models with and without fibers perform at 15 fps, with the tetrahedral mesh consisting of 5664 tetrahedra and 2064 nodes (including 16 fixed nodes).

Muscular tissue is a typical example of transversely isotropic materials, whose mechanical response is controlled by the internal muscle fibers. For example, the beating movement of the heart is controlled by the regular periodic contraction of the myocardium. Using the fiber-guided model, we can simulate the complex movements of the heart beating. To further explore the application of our fiber-field incorporated FEM model for more complex topological structures, we conduct an investigation with a heart which possesses two chambers and contracting muscles.

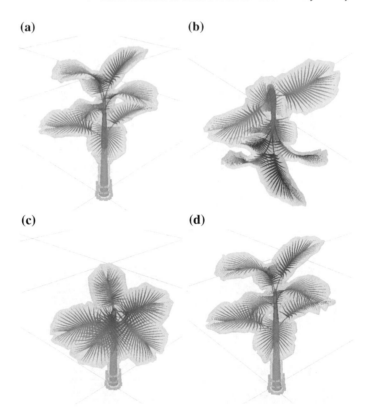

Fig. 4.5 Deformations of different FEM models under gravity: **a** original shape; **b** homogeneous and isotropic material; **c** heterogeneous and isotropic materials; **d** fiber-field incorporated model, with heterogeneous and isotropic materials

A screenshot of the beating heart is shown at left in Fig. 4.7a, and its corresponding fiber-field vectors are displayed in Fig. 4.7b.

4.5.3 Validation

We show that isotropic materials can be dealt with as a special case by our *fiber-field incorporated model*; the same deformations by the existing *isotropic FEM model* can be reproduced by our model. In Fig. 4.8a, the deformed result of an isotropic rectangular bar under gravity is represented by the tetrahedral mesh computed by the existing CLFEM model. In Fig. 4.8b, the fiber field is generated for the isotropic material by our new model, which preserves the same deformation of the tetrahedral mesh. In contrast, we can redefine the fiber in the same FEM model for an anisotropic material to view its effect. Figure 4.8c shows the deformed results of a transversely isotropic material under gravity (with smaller stretching

(a)   **(b)**

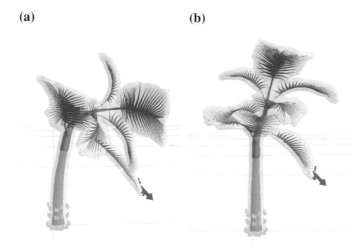

Fig. 4.6 Deformations under a dragging force. **a** without fiber; **b** fiber-field incorporated model

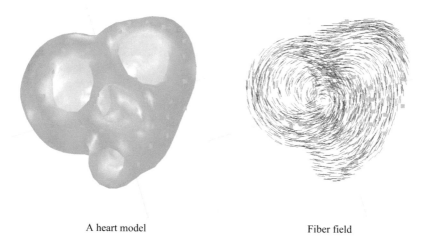

A heart model   Fiber field

Fig. 4.7 A beating heart simulation using our fiber-field incorporated FEM model Conclusion (fiber-field generated by [TAKAYAMA '08])

resistance along the fiber directions), which clearly illustrate the different fiber field from that in Fig. 4.1b and the different tetrahedral mesh from those in Fig. 4.8a, b.

Quantitative Comparison For isotropic materials, mechanical response is independent of directions in the material space. Thus theoretically, the local frame transformations in our model will not affect its behaviors and should produce exactly the same results, i.e. displacement field u. To validate this, we give a quantitative comparison of the two models in Fig. 4.8a, b. The bar model in Fig. 4.8a has 311 vertices (1039 elements), with 20 fixed vertices; that is, the degree

(a)   **(b)**   **(c)**

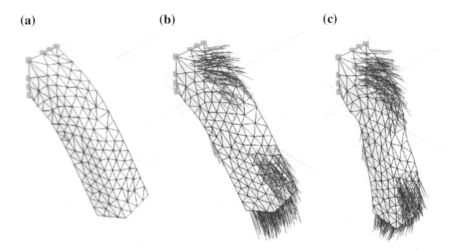

Fig. 4.8 Validation of the correctness of the fiber-field incorporated models. **a** CLFEM for isotropic material; **b** Fiber incorporation for isotropic material; **c** Fiber incorporation for anisotropic material

of freedom is 873. We compare the displacement field and of the two simulations at equilibrium, using the square difference formula $diff := \sum_i (\mathbf{u}_{1i} - \mathbf{u}_{2i})^2$. The computed difference is 3.95e−012, resulting in the same $\mathbf{u}_1$ and $\mathbf{u}_2$. Thus, we have quantitatively validated the correctness of our fiber-field incorporated model for the special case of isotropic material.

4.6 Summary

In previous work, physically-plausible deformable models have been developed mainly for isotropic materials. We have presented a novel fiber-field incorporated FEM model to deal with transversely isotropic anisotropic materials. The key idea is to use a fiber-field to establish local element coordinate frames, and to formulate a corotational linear FEM model based on local frames. For simulation in virtual surgery, our fiber-field incorporated models can yield realistic deformations. The main advantages of our model are:

i. Rather than computing additional strain energy of embedded fibers as in the conventional fiber-reinforced models, we only use the orientation information to form a fiber field.

ii. The fiber-field incorporated model is based on corotational linear FEM model, which is more computational efficient than nonlinear FEM models, and large deformations can be accommodated.

iii. Additional computation in the proposed model can be done by pre-computation, thus no additional cost is added during simulation.

A more flexible user interface for fiber generation and material parameter adjustment tools are yet to develop. In specific applications, this orientation field can be generated from Diffusion Tensor MRI (DTMRI) techniques when muscular tissues are acquired (e.g., [12, 13]) for more accurate mechanical and physiological analysis. In the future, this idea can be further extended to simulate other kinds of anisotropy, such as orthotropic materials, given a local frame which can represent different material plane symmetries.

Notes: The sketch-based interface is implemented with reference to *Kenshi's* paper [10].

References

1. Ogden, R. (2003) *Nonlinear elasticity, anisotropy, material stability and residual stresses in soft tissue* (pp. 65–108). Courses And Lectures-International Centre For Mechanical Sciences.
2. Picinbono, G., Delingette, H., & Ayache, N. (2001) *Nonlinear and anisotropic elastic soft tissue models for medical simulation*. IEEE.
3. Picinbono, G., Delingette, H., & Ayache, N. (2003). Non-linear anisotropic elasticity for real-time surgery simulation. *Graphical Models, 65*(5), 305–321.
4. Irving, G., Teran, J., & Fedkiw, R. (2004) Invertible finite elements for robust simulation of large deformation. In *Proceedings of the 2004 ACM SIGGRAPH/Eurographics Symposium on Computer Animation* (pp. 131–140). Grenoble, France: Eurographics Association.
5. Teran, J., et al. (2003) Finite volume methods for the simulation of skeletal muscle. In *Proceedings of the 2003 ACM SIGGRAPH/Eurographics Symposium on Computer Animation* (pp. 68–74). San Diego, California: Eurographics Association.
6. Liu, N., et al. (2012) Physical material editing with structure embedding for animated solid. In *Proceedings of Graphics Interface 2012* (pp. 193–200). Toronto, Ontario, Canada: Canadian Information Processing Society.
7. Ting, T. C. T. (1996). *Anisotropic elasticity: Theory and applications* (Vol. 45). USA: Oxford University Press.
8. Müller, M., & Gross, M. (2004) Interactive virtual materials, In *Proceedings of Graphics Interface* (pp. 239–246). London, Ontario, Canada: Canadian Human-Computer Communications Society.
9. Baraff, D., & Witkin, A. (1998) Large steps in cloth simulation. In *Proceedings of the 25th annual conference on Computer graphics and interactive techniques* (pp. 43–54). ACM.
10. Takayama, K., et al. (2008). A sketch-based interface for modeling myocardial fiber orientation that considers the layered structure of the ventricles. *The Journal of Physiological Sciences: JPS, 58*(7), 487–492.
11. Ijiri, T., et al. (2012). A kinematic approach for efficient and robust simulation of the cardiac beating motion. *PLoS ONE, 7*(5), e36706.
12. Rohmer, D., Sitek, A., & Gullberg, G. T. (2007). Reconstruction and visualization of fiber and laminar structure in the normal human heart from ex vivo diffusion tensor magnetic resonance imaging (DTMRI) data. *Investigative Radiology, 42*(11), 777.
13. Sosnovik, D. E., et al. (2009). Diffusion MR tractography of the heart. *Journal of Cardiovascular Magnetic Resonance, 11*(1), 1–15.

Chapter 5
Dynamics Controls for Orthotropic Materials

Abstract In this chapter, we further introduce deformation simulation for orthotropic materials. An orthotropic deformation controlling *frame-field* is conceptualized and a frame construction tool is developed for users to define the desired material properties. A quaternion Laplacian smoothing algorithm is designed for propagating the user-defined sparsely distributed frames into the entire object. The orthotropic frame-field is coupled with the CLFEM model to complete an orthotropic deformable model.

5.1 Introduction

In Chap. 4, we studied transversely isotropic materials and developed a *fiber-field incorporated FEM model*. Here, we further investigate orthotropic materials.

As a special class of anisotropic materials, orthotropic materials exhibit different mechanical behaviors along three orthogonal directions. They have more degrees-of-freedom with material properties than transversely isotropic materials, and can generate more complex mechanical behaviors. Therefore, it requires careful adjustment of material parameters to ensure numerical stability.

Most of the existing physically-based deformable models in the literature are mainly based on the assumption of isotropic materials, such as the *St.Venant-Kirchhoff* material and the *Neo-Hookean* material. In terms of anisotropy, transversely isotropic materials are often discussed in existing work, and a review can be found in the Chap. 4. To date, modeling methods for simulation of deformable objects with orthotropic materials are little discussed; and there is a lack of intuition in designing orthotropic models in graphics applications.

We proposed a solution here for modeling and deformation control of orthotropic deformable objects.

- Firstly, constraints of material properties with respect to the strain energy density are analyzed, and a positive-definite elasticity tensor is derived for an orthotropic material.

© Springer International Publishing Switzerland 2016
J. Cai et al., *Graphical Simulation of Deformable Models*,
DOI 10.1007/978-3-319-51031-6_5

- Secondly, an orthotropic deformation controlling frame-field is conceptualized and a frame construction tool is developed for users to define the desired material properties. Rotation minimizing frames along with several user-defined NURBS curves are propagated into the entire body of the deformable object, forming a frame-field. A quaternion Laplacian smoothing algorithm is developed for generating such a smooth frame-field.
- Thirdly, the corotational linear FEM (CLFEM) model coupled with the orthonormal frame-field is formulated to realize a dynamics simulation system, which is computationally efficient and supports large deformations.

All the algorithms have been implemented in a modeling and simulation system, and a GUI is provided to design the orthotropic model. Experiments on real-time dynamics simulation and analytical comparisons are presented.

5.2   Related Work

In terms of anisotropy, transversely isotropic materials are often researched in computer graphics area, as discussed in the last chapter. However, orthotropic models are less discussed. Li et al. [1] proposed a stable way to tune the complicated material properties for anisotropic materials. There is lack of approaches for intuitive deformation controls.

We aim at a more effective deformation control method. In previous research, *example-based* methods and *space-time control* methods have been proposed to provide users with intuitive art-directed control of complex anisotropic behaviors; a review of these approaches can be found in Error! Reference source not found. However, these deformation controls achieve anisotropy by adding artificial forces that violate physics rules.

Inspired by our first work that incorporates a *fiber-field* for transversely isotropic materials, we propose a *frame-field* incorporated deformation control here. We provide a novel interactive tool to generate a frame-field for orthotropic materials, which is coupled with a corotational FEM model. Our method can control the orthotropic behaviors and make the deformations more predictable.

5.3   Computational Model of Orthotropic Materials

5.3.1   Elasticity Tensor of Orthotropic Materials

In contrast to a transversely isotropic material that has preferred material directions (as described previously in Sect. 4.2), an orthotropic material has three mutually orthogonal planes of rotational symmetry. It exhibits different stiffness along these three orthogonal directions, and has *nine* independent parameters. The symmetric elasticity tensor C is defined as

$$C = \begin{bmatrix} A & 0 \\ 0 & B \end{bmatrix},$$ (5.1)

where

$$A = \gamma \begin{bmatrix} E_1(1 - v_{23}v_{32}) & E_1(v_{21} + v_{23}v_{31}) & E_1(v_{31} + v_{21}v_{32}) \\ E_2(v_{12} + v_{13}v_{32}) & E_2(1 - v_{13}v_{31}) & E_2(v_{32} + v_{12}v_{31}) \\ E_3(v_{13} + v_{12}v_{23}) & E_3(v_{23} + v_{13}v_{21}) & E_3(1 - v_{12}v_{21}) \end{bmatrix},$$

$$B = \begin{bmatrix} \mu_{23} & 0 & 0 \\ 0 & \mu_{31} & 0 \\ 0 & 0 & \mu_{12} \end{bmatrix},$$

$\gamma = \frac{1}{1 - v_{12}v_{21} - v_{23}v_{32} - v_{31}v_{13} - 2v_{21}v_{32}v_{13}}$, and we have $v_{21}v_{32}v_{13} = v_{12}v_{23}v_{31}$.

From the above, we need to determine 9 independent parameters:

- 3 Young's moduli E_1, E_2, E_3, along three orthogonal principal axes respectively;
- 6 Poisson's ratios v_{ij}, $(i \neq j)$, satisfying that $v_{ij}/E_i = v_{ji}/E_j$, so only 3 independent degrees-of-freedom remain;
- 3 shear moduli $\mu_{12}, \mu_{23}, \mu_{31}$ on three principal planes.

The inverse elasticity tensor, $S = C^{-1}$, can be derived and be represented by a relatively simple form as follows

$$S = \begin{bmatrix} \frac{1}{E_1} & -\frac{v_{21}}{E_2} & -\frac{v_{31}}{E_3} & 0 & 0 & 0 \\ -\frac{v_{12}}{E_1} & \frac{1}{E_2} & -\frac{v_{32}}{E_3} & 0 & 0 & 0 \\ -\frac{v_{13}}{E_1} & -\frac{v_{23}}{E_2} & \frac{1}{E_3} & 0 & 0 & 0 \\ 0 & 0 & 0 & \frac{1}{\mu_{23}} & 0 & 0 \\ 0 & 0 & 0 & 0 & \frac{1}{\mu_{31}} & 0 \\ 0 & 0 & 0 & 0 & 0 & \frac{1}{\mu_{12}} \end{bmatrix},$$

which is a simpler form than that of C, and can be used for the positive-definiteness analysis in the following section.

5.3.2   Computation for Strain Energy Density

The strain energy density is defined by

$$\psi(\varepsilon) \;=\; \frac{1}{2}\sigma^T\varepsilon \;=\; \frac{1}{2}\varepsilon^T C\varepsilon \;=\; \frac{1}{2}\sigma^T S\sigma, \tag{5.2}$$

Here ψ should be made a positive-definite function of ε (or, σ); it is equivalent to require that C (or S, equivalently) be positive-definite. According to the *Sylvester's criterion* that a real symmetric matrix is positive-definite if all its principal minors are positive, parameters of an orthotropic material should satisfy the following conditions:

$$
\begin{aligned}
&E_1,\ E_2,\ E_3 > 0,\\
&\mu_{12},\ \mu_{23},\ \mu_{31} > 0,\\
&v_{12}v_{21} < 1,\ v_{23}v_{32} < 1,\ v_{13}v_{31} < 1,\ \gamma > 0.
\end{aligned}
\tag{5.3}
$$

Li et al. [1] proposed a strategy to reduce the number of material parameters to 4. Although the simplified set cannot express the entire family of orthotropic materials, it helps animators stably tune the material properties.

However, the previous work lacks a spatial definition of principal axes for an orthotropic model. Li et al. [1] considered directional derivatives of a 3D texture map, but this suggests the use of a complex tool for designing 3D texture maps. To solve this problem, we propose a user-guided tool for defining a spatially varying *frame-field* in the following section.

5.4   Model Control with Spatially Varying Frame-Field

As discussed above, orthotropic materials exhibit different stiffnesses along different directions, and the material parameters are specified in a frame of principal axes. Therefore, for the simulated mesh (tetrahedral mesh in our study) of a deformable model, a local frame needs to be assigned for each element, which forms a spatially varying *frame-field*.

Our goal here is to design an interactive and intuitive tool to generate such a frame-field that helps to specify material properties and control the orthotropic deformation behaviors in a more predictable way. A relevant work by Choi et al. [2] proposed a numerical representation of fascicle trajectories of skeletal muscle, using the gradient of a smooth scalar field generated by heat diffusion. The scalar field is obtained by solving a Laplacian equation using the finite volume method. Our work in the Sect. 4.2 proposed an FEM model augmented with a smooth vector-field (i.e., fiber-field) to simulate transversely isotropic materials. Similar in spirit, however, here an *orthonormal* frame-field is formed for orthotropic models.

The main idea of our proposed approach is that:

(1) Firstly, the user forms some smooth curves upon the TET mesh, by only putting control points on the mesh surface. The NURBS curves are generated according to the control points, which indicate a fibrous structure of the shape,

and a series of orthonormal frames are generated simultaneously along the curves, forming a sparse distribution of frames.

(2) Then, a frame-field is automatically generated by a smooth interpolation of the sparse frames, which consists of local frames for all the TET elements.

(3) Finally, this frame-field is augmented with the corotational FEM model to formulate an orthotropic model.

Detailed algorithms with respect to the three steps are presented separately in this section.

5.4.1 Rotation Minimizing Frames as the Indication of Material Principal Axes

Let $x(u) = (x(u), y(u), z(u))$ be a C^1 regular curve in 3D Euclidean space $\mathbb{E}^3$, its unit tangent vector can be computed as $(u) = \frac{x'}{\|x'\|}$, where $x' = \frac{dx}{du}$. Then a *moving frame* associated with the curve can be defined as an orthonormal system composed of a tangent vector and two orthogonal vectors on a normal plane at the current position.

The *Frenet* frame $(t(u), n(u), b(u))$ is a familiar example from differential geometry, where $b = (x' \times x'')/\|x' \times x''\|$ and $= b \times t$. However, the Frenet frame is not a suitable choice here, due to its '*unnecessary rotation*' in the curve normal plane and lack of controllability.

With convenient and intuitive control as our first concern, we employ the NURBS curves and associated *rotation minimizing frames*, to generate a sparse distribution of orthonormal frames, which will be further used for interpolation.

5.4.1.1 A Recap of Rotation Minimizing Frames

A *rotation minimizing frame* (RMF) [3] does not rotate about the instantaneous tangent of the curve, meaning that among all moving frames on a space curve the RMF yields least elastic energy associated with twisting.

A definition by differential equations is as follows: given a C^1 curve $x(u) \in \mathbb{E}^3$ and its unit tangent vector $t(u)$, a moving frame $(r(u), s(u), t(u))$, where $r(u) \times s(u) = t(u)$, is called a *rotation minimizing frame* if $r(u)$ satisfies the following system of differential algebraic equations (DAE) [4]:

$$\begin{cases} r'(u) - \phi(u)t(u) = \mathbf{0}, \\ r(u) \cdot t(u) = 0 \end{cases},$$

where $\phi(u)$ is some scalar function. Such a vector function $r(u)$ perpendicular to the tangent vector exhibits minimal rotation, it is thus called a *rotation minimizing vector*. $r(u)$ is not necessarily differentiable for a C^1 curve, thus an adapted *weak form* of the DAE can be defined as

$$\begin{cases} r'(u) - \int_0^u \phi(v)\, t(u) dv = \mathbf{0} \\ r(u) \cdot t(u) = 0 \end{cases}.$$

5.4.1.2 RMFs Associated with NURBS Curves

RMFs are commonly used in sweep surface modeling and path planning of animations. However, here we choose the RMFs associated with NURBS curves as the constraints for generating material principal axes, which to some extent can be considered as an indication of the material distribution of an orthotropic model: tangent direction of the curve is represented as one principal axis, and thus a corresponding RMF is denoted as a local material frame.

An example is shown in Fig. 5.1. A third-degree NURBS curve is chosen here for its smoothness and controllability. Note that only the two end-nodes of the control points are interpolated and the in-between ones are extrapolated. This can be useful for tolerance of bumpy surfaces. The NURBS curves intuitively imply the main structures of the orthotropic object, which is similar to shape medial-lines or fiber direction of a fibrous object.

We choose the RMF for its nice properties that are desirable features in design, as follows:

(1) The RMF is stable, unlike the Frenet frame that leads to undesirable twists in motion along a general curve; and its *minimal twist property* reflects the natural structure of an object, e.g., fibers of muscle or a tree.
(2) The RMF is easy to control. The user can simply manipulate the orientation of the RMFs by changing the orientation of the first frame, causing the following

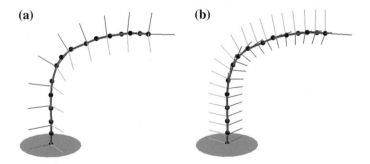

Fig. 5.1 The orientation of the RMFs can be adjusted by changing the orientation of the first frame. The 2D-disk, which is orthogonal to the *blue* axis of the first frame and contains the other two axes (*red* and *green*), is an intuitive display of the orientation of the first frame

frames to be changed accordingly (due to the minimal twist property), as shown in Fig. 5.1. The number of frames generated can be set on-the-fly as well.

Exact computation of the RMFs is either impractical or computationally expensive. The *double reflection* method based on the discrete approximation proposed by Wang et al. [4] is used here. It is stable, efficient and accurate (with fourth order global approximation error). All the design and manipulations can be done at an interactive rate.

5.4.2   Laplacian Smoothing of the RMFs

Our goal now is to generate a frame-field (e.g., as in Fig. 5.3) for a TET mesh with the obtained sparsely distributed RMFs (as in Fig. 5.2).

Given a global coordinate system, orthogonal frame of the RMFs can be directly represented by a 3×3 matrix,

$$Q_i = (r_{i1}, r_{i2}, r_{i3}), \quad i = 0, \ldots, m, \tag{5.4}$$

where m is the total number of the RMFs, (r_{i1}, r_{i2}, r_{i3}) are the coordinate-vectors of the three axes respectively (as column vectors). Q_i^T can be considered as a rotation

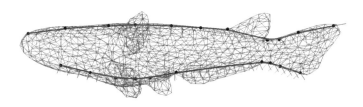

Fig. 5.2 The user plots some control points (the *black* dots) on the surface of the simulated mesh, then the NURBS curves (in *purple*) and associated RMFs are automatically generated (the *RGB* colored orthotropic frames)

Fig. 5.3 The frame-field is generated by Laplacian smoothing of the RMFs associated with the NURBS curves

matrix that transforms a vector from the global frame to a local frame. Therefore, the task here turns into a problem of interpolation of rotations, which is commonly used in animation and skinning methods.

An early and simple solution is the *linear blend skinning* (LBS) [5]. It essentially does a linear element-wise interpolation of rotation matrices that is computationally efficient; however, it leads to non-rotations and thus suffers volume-collapse artifacts. The *spherical linear interpolation* (SLERP) [6] works well for blending two rotations, using quaternions to represent rotations, but it cannot be directly applied in a scenario involving more than two rotations. A fast approximate *quaternion linear blending* (QLERP) [7] uses a simple linear quaternion averaging of multiple quaternions and re-normalization. It offers reasonable skinning results with low time and memory complexity. There are also advanced skinning methods, such as *dual-quaternion blending* [8], which blend rigid transformations including not only rotations but also translations, and achieves better skinning results than the former methods. With only rotations involved in our task, an essentially linear interpolation scheme of quaternions is employed here for the generation of the desired frame-field. An advantage of this linear combination is that it is computationally efficient, which is important for interactive design.

Instead of using a blending scheme as in skinning, a Laplacian smoothing method [9, 10] is exploited here. A big advantage of this approach is that a complicated weight function (such as *radial basis function, biharmonic weights* [11]) or a labor-intensive weight-painting is not required to define vertex weights, which is a prerequisite for the previous method. Weights are defined based on Euclidean distances between neighboring elements. With an intuitive geometric meaning, this method relieves a user of a laborious task. It is computationally efficient, producing results sufficient for the task here.

5.4.2.1 Formulation of Quaternion Laplacian

Quaternions are used as representations for local frames. Each frame Q_i is firstly converted to a quaternion representation $\boldsymbol{q}_i = (\theta_i, x_i, y_i, z_i)$. The Laplacian smoothing is performed on the TET elements for the interpolation of the quaternions, with the RMFs as the constraints. We do the Laplacian smoothing on each θ-, x-, y-, z-component respectively, and finally obtain the frame-field by conversion of the resulting quaternions. Here we formulate the Laplacian method via the θ-component, and perform the same processing on the other three components (x, y, and z).

The **Laplacian** based on the quaternion component is defined as

$$\delta_i = \sum_{j \in N_{r_i}} \omega_j^i \theta_j - \theta_i, \qquad i = 1, \ldots, n, \tag{5.5}$$

where n is the total number of elements, and N_{r_i} is the index set of the neighboring elements of the ith element. Here, we choose the face-sharing neighbors, which form a smaller set than the vertex-sharing neighbors and thus need less computation. ω_j^i represents the weight defined as

$$\omega_j^i = \frac{exp(-d_{ij}^2)}{\sum_{k \in N_{r_i}} exp(-d_{ik}^2)}, \tag{5.6}$$

where d_{ij} is the Euclidean distance between two neighboring elements (here we use the distance between their centroids).

The constraints of the Laplacian smoothing are set for the elements near the RMFs, as

$$\sum_{j \in \bar{N}_{r_i}} \bar{\omega}_j^i \theta_j = \bar{\theta}_i, \qquad i = 1, \ldots, m, \tag{5.7}$$

where m is the total number of RMF frames, $\bar{\theta}_i$ is the known component of the ith quaternion (i.e., corresponding to the ith RMF frame), and $\bar{N}_{r_i}$ is the index set of the elements close to the position of the ith frame, and the weight $\bar{\omega}_j^i$ is defined similarly to Eq. (5.6), as

$$\bar{\omega}_j^i = \frac{exp(-\bar{d}_{ij})}{\sum_{k \in N_{r_i}} exp(-\bar{d}_{ij})} \tag{5.8}$$

where $\bar{d}_{ij}$ is the Euclidean distance between the centroid of an element and the origin of a frame.

This Laplacian smoothing problem, with the definition of Laplacian in Eq. (5.5) and the constraint in Eq. (5.7), can be formulated in a matrix form respectively, as

$$\begin{aligned} \boldsymbol{\delta} &= L\boldsymbol{\theta}, & \boldsymbol{\delta} &= (\delta_1, \ldots, \delta_n)^T, \boldsymbol{\theta} = (\theta_1 \ldots, \theta_n)^T, \\ \bar{C}\boldsymbol{\theta} &= \bar{\boldsymbol{\theta}}, & \bar{\boldsymbol{\theta}} &= (\bar{\theta}_1 \ldots, \bar{\theta}_m)^T, \end{aligned} \tag{5.9}$$

where $L_{ij} = \begin{cases} -1, & j = i \\ \omega_j^i, & j \in N_{r_i} \\ 0, & otherwise \end{cases}$ and $C_{ij} = \begin{cases} \bar{\omega}_j^i, & j \in \bar{N}_{r_i} \\ 0, & otherwise \end{cases}$.

Thus, $L \in \mathbb{R}^{n \times n}$ and $\bar{C} \in \mathbb{R}^{m \times n}$, where usually $m \ll n$, i.e., the constrained elements are a small set of the TET mesh.

5.4.2.2   Solving a Minimization Problem

The Laplacian smoothing process can be formulated as a minimization problem,

$$\min_{\theta} \left\| \begin{pmatrix} L \\ \bar{C} \end{pmatrix} \theta - \begin{pmatrix} 0 \\ \bar{\theta} \end{pmatrix} \right\|_2^2, \qquad (5.10)$$

where $\|\bullet\|$ is the L-2 norm. This formulation implies that the quaternion-components of an element should be a linear combination of those of its neighbors, and some of them are constrained by the user-defined RMFs. With the above formulation, both of the conditions are satisfied in a least squares sense. Solving the quadratic minimization problem in Eq. (5.10) is equivalent to solving a sparse linear system:

$$A^T A \theta = A^T b, \qquad (5.11)$$

where

$$A = \begin{pmatrix} L \\ \bar{C} \end{pmatrix} \; and \; b = \begin{pmatrix} 0 \\ \bar{\theta} \end{pmatrix}.$$

Furthermore, we have the $n \times n$ sparse symmetric system matrix and the right hand side in (5.11) are computed as

$$A^T A = L^T L + \bar{C}^T \bar{C},$$
$$A^T b = \bar{C}^T \bar{\theta}.$$

Here, $L^T L$ is a constant matrix that can be pre-computed.

The Laplacian smoothing is done on the four quaternion-components separately, meaning that four linear equations with the same system matrix are to be solved. Therefore, a direct linear system solver, which performs LU factorization of the system matrix only once and then solves the four equations independently, would be a good choice here. The UMFPACK library [12] is used here. The direct solver performs very fast due to pre-factorization of the system matrix. It takes much more time to prepare the sparse matrices L and $\bar{C}$, involving neighbors search, weights computation and sparse matrices construction, which is the performance bottle-neck in our un-optimized implementation.

The above Laplacian smoothing performs an element-wise method, i.e., quaternions are computed for the elements directly. An alternative is to compute the quaternion at each vertex, and then obtain the element quaternions by barycentric interpolation. The vertex-wise approach usually reduces computation, since in most cases the number of vertices is smaller than that of the elements; for example, the TET mesh of the raptor model in Fig. 5.5 contains 2996 vertices and 8148 elements. For the raptor model, the vertex-wise method takes about 367 ms to prepare the matrices and 32 ms to solve all the linear equations, while the element-wise one takes about 1665 ms and 52 ms respectively. An effective way to improve performance is to pre-compute $L^T L$ and only to update the $\bar{C}$ related computation on-the-fly.

In conclusion, the RMF generation involving user interaction can be done in real-time, and for a TET mesh with tens of thousands of elements the frame-field generation takes a few seconds, which is acceptable as a data preparation phase in the simulation system; and the generated frame-field can be stored in an off-line file.

5.4.3 Simulation of Orthotropic Deformable Models

The corotational FEM (CLFEM) model (as described in Sect. 4.3) is also used here to support large deformations, and augment it with a frame-field to deliver orthotropic behaviors. Similar to the idea of fiber-field incorporated model in the last chapter, we augment the CLFEM with the frame-field, in a way that the internal force is computed in the local frames instead of the single global frame, as

$$f^e_{int} = R^e Q^e \widehat{f}^e_{int} = R^e Q^e \widehat{K^e} Q^{e^T} (R^{e^T} x - X) = R^e K^e \left(R^{e^T} x - X \right),$$

The element stiffness matrix becomes $K^e = Q^e K^e Q^{e^T}$. Through cumbersome algebra, K^e here is essentially equivalent to the stiffness matrix used in the paper [1] (or, refer to [13] for more details). However, here we present and compute it in a more easily comprehensive way. Due to the fact that Q^e is pre-computed, K^e can also be pre-computed. Therefore, in our frame-field augmented approach, no additional computational cost is introduced into the CLFEM simulation.

For the dynamics simulation, the equations of motion are solved by an *implicit backward Euler* integration with a conjugate gradient solver.

5.5 Experiments and Discussions

In this section, we validate the effectiveness of our proposed modeling approach using some typical models, and compare the deformations of isotropic and orthotropic materials. The same external loads including gravity and directional pulling force are applied to both the isotropic and the orthotropic models.

5.5.1 Orthotropic FEM Dynamics

In the following experiments, the tetrahedral meshes are rendered in wire-frame mode to reveal the model structures, and a surface mesh of high resolution, which is deformed by the tetrahedral mesh by interpolation, is embedded for better visual effects in the final renderings. The green dots denote the constraint vertices that are fixed in positions, and the red arrows represent the external directional force applied onto the selected vertices. In the descriptions, we denote r, g and b-axis as the three principal axes in the frame-field.

For more robust simulation, the invertible elasticity approach [14] is applied to deal with degenerate and inverted elements during simulation.

In the first experiment, referring to Fig. 5.4, we use the fish model which represents a typical structure with a simple topology. We have used it to illustrate the generation of the frame-field in the previous sections. We present the comparison of the isotropic and the orthotropic deformations under three directional forces. The first column screenshots show the isotropic deformations and the second column shows the corresponding orthotropic deformations under the same directional force.

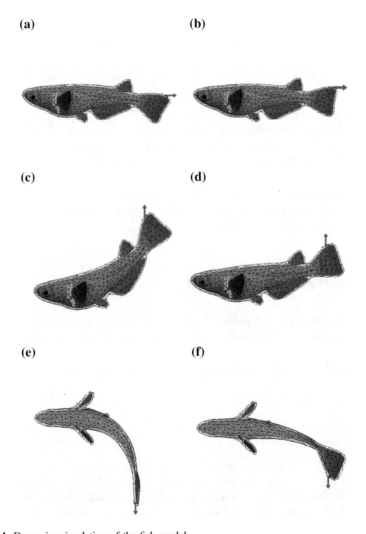

Fig. 5.4 Dynamics simulation of the fish model

(a)   **(b)**

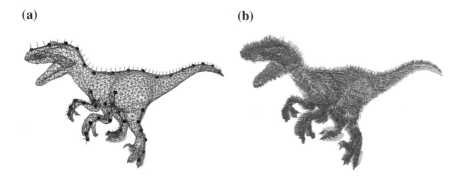

Fig. 5.5 a Multiple RMFs for a raptor model, **b** The frame-field with the Laplacian smoothing

In this experiment, we define an orthotropic material with stiffness of $0.1\times$ $1.0\times$, and $10.0\times$ times of that of the isotropic material along the respective *r*-, *g*- and *b*-axis directions in the frame-field, highlighted features are:

- In the pair of Fig. 5.4a, b, the orthotropic model in the latter shows the desired resistance against a stretch along the longitudinal direction ($10.0\times$ in b-axis). It avoids the incorrect geometric deformation commonly seen in the isotropic model as the former.
- In the pair of Fig. 5.4c, d, due to the increased stiffness from $1.0\times$ to $10.0\times$ in the b-axis of the latter, pulling the tail makes it bend upwards but the fish body is not wrongly elongated as in the former. This behavior matches with the dynamics of vertebrate animals.
- In the pair of Fig. 5.4e, f, due to the decreased stiffness from $1.0\times$ to $0.1\times$ in the r-axis of the latter, pulling a corner of the tail makes a realistic twisting deformation which cannot be achieved in the former.

In the second experiment, referring to Figs. 5.5 and 5.6, we use a raptor model with more complex structures. We verify the controllability of multiple RMFs and the effectiveness of the Laplacian smoothing in defining an orthotropic material.

In this experiment, we also define an orthotropic material with stiffness of $0.1\times$, $1.0\times$ and $10.0\times$ times of that of the isotropic material along the respective *r*-, *g*- and *b*-axis in the frame-field. If the isotropic model is set as a soft material, the raptor model cannot stand on its feet under gravity (as shown in Fig. 5.6a, acting like boneless soft body; or if set as a stiff material that $10.0\times$ times of the one in Fig. 5.6a, it lacks of flexibility in other directions (as shown in Fig. 5.6c under the directional force). In contrast, the orthotropic model shows the expected deformations under both gravity and the external force (as shown in Fig. 5.6b, d, which reflect to certain extent their internal structures.

In the last experiment, referring to Figs. 5.7 and 5.8, we use a hosta plant model with structures of heterogeneous materials (soft leaves and stiff stems) to

(a)   (b)

(c)   (d)

Fig. 5.6 Dynamics simulation of the raptor model

verify the effectiveness of the orthotropic model in combination with the stiffness matrices.

For references, we present two views of the rest poses of the hosta plant model in the first row of Fig. 5.8. Highlighted features in this experiment are:

(a)   **(b)**

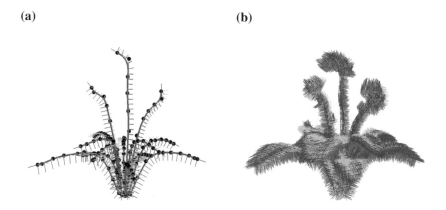

Fig. 5.7 **a** Multiple RMFs for a hosta plant model, **b** The frame-field with Laplacian smoothing

- In the second row of Fig. 5.8, the model of isotropic materials lacks varying stiffness in different parts, thus is pulled down uniformly by the gravity in Fig. 5.8c and freely bent by the directional pulling force in Fig. 5.8d.
- In the orthotropic model of the third row, we define different stiffness for the leaves and other parts, that is, $0.2\times$, $1.0\times$ and $10.0\times$ times of the isotropic material for the leaves, and $1.0\times$, $1.0\times$ and $10.0\times$ times for the others parts, along r-, g- and b-axis respectively. As expected, the heterogeneous orthotropic model well approximates the natural deformations of the plant model. Under the gravity and directional pulling force, the greater stiffness along its longitudinal direction tends to resist the deformation from the rest status. Meanwhile, the leaves with less stiffness exhibit the flexibility in deformation along the other directions, as shown in Fig. 5.8e, f.

To validate its consistent performance as in the isotropic model with CLFEM, we implement our algorithms for the orthotropic model on the same platform. The frames-per-second (FPS) performance of the dynamics simulation in the three experiments is given in Table 5.1.

As can be seen, it is verified that there is no additional computational cost for the orthotropic deformations compared with the isotropic ones.

5.6 Summary

Modeling the anisotropic materials is highly desired but has been proven to be a challenging task. In this paper, we have studied the orthotropic materials, and proposed a deformable object modeling and dynamics simulation method for orthotropic materials of a wide range of objects such as animals and plants. Technical innovations are made in several aspects:

(a)   (b)

(c)   (d)

(e)   (f)

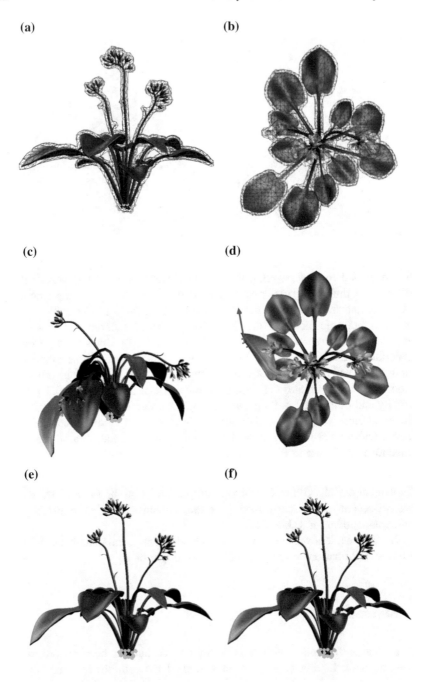

Fig. 5.8 Dynamics simulation of the hosta plant model

Table 5.1 Simulation performance

	Vertices	Tets	FPS (Iso)	FPS (Ortho)
Fish	1114	4081	40	40
Raptor	2296	8418	21	21
Hosta	3367	9512	18	18

i. An orthotropic deformation controlling frame-field is conceptualized and the frame construction tool is developed for the user to define the desired material properties. Moreover, a quaternion Laplacian smoothing algorithm is designed for propagating the sparse and distributed frames to the entire object.
ii. To enable large anisotropic deformations, the orthotropic frame-field is coupled with the CLFEM model. In this way, we can complete a dynamics system for use in physically based deformation simulation.

To verify the effectiveness of the proposed algorithms, we have developed a comprehensive modeling and simulation system, and conducted experiments on real-time deformation simulation. Our analytical comparisons of isotropic and orthotropic materials in deformation behaviors have confirmed good real-time performance.

Though our model can couple with CLFEM for large deformations, and the degenerate and inverted cases can be handled properly in most cases, more restricted time step is required for scenarios where the anisotropy is increasing, that is, there are large differences among stiffnesses along the material axes. We propose further study on general nonlinear orthotropic models in the future.

References

1. Li, Y., et al. (2014). Stable orthotropic materials. In *Proceedings of the ACM SIGGRAPH/Eurographics Symposium on Computer Animation*. Eurographics Association.
2. Choi, H. F., & Blemker, S. S. (2013). Skeletal muscle fascicle arrangements can be reconstructed using a laplacian vector field simulation. *PLoS ONE, 8*(10), e77576.
3. Bloomenthal, M. (1988). *Approximation of sweep surfaces by tensor product B-splines*. Tech Reports UUCS-88-008, University of Utah.
4. Wang, W., et al. (2008). Computation of rotation minimizing frames. *ACM Transactions on Graphics (TOG), 27*(1), 2.
5. Magnenat-Thalmann, N., Laperrire, R., & Thalmann, D. (1988). Joint-dependent local deformations for hand animation and object grasping. In *Proceedings on Graphics Interface '88*. Citeseer.
6. Shoemake, K. (1985). Animating rotation with quaternion curves. In *ACM SIGGRAPH Computer Graphics*. ACM.
7. Kavan, L., & Žára, J. (2005). Spherical blend skinning: A real-time deformation of articulated models. In *Proceedings of the 2005 Symposium on Interactive 3D Graphics and Games*. ACM.
8. Kavan, L., et al. (2006). *Dual quaternions for rigid transformation blending*. Trinity College Dublin, Tech. Rep. TCD-CS-2006-46.

9. Sorkine, O., et al. (2004). Laplacian surface editing. In *Proceedings of the 2004 Eurographics/ACM SIGGRAPH Symposium on Geometry Processing*. ACM.
10. Takayama, K., et al. (2007). A sketch-based interface for modeling myocardial fiber orientation. In *Smart graphics*. Berlin: Springer.
11. Lipman, Y., Rustamov, R. M., & Funkhouser, T. A. (2010). Biharmonic distance. *ACM Transactions on Graphics (TOG), 29*(3), 27.
12. Davis, T. A. (2004). UMFPACK-an unsymmetric-pattern multifrontal method with a column pre-ordering strategy. *ACM Transactions on Mathematical Software (TOMS), 30*(204), 196–199.
13. Bower, A. F. (2009). *Applied mechanics of solids*. Boca Raton: CRC press.
14. Irving, G., Teran, J., & Fedkiw, R. (2004). Invertible finite elements for robust simulation of large deformation. In *Proceedings of the 2004 ACM SIGGRAPH/Eurographics Symposium on Computer Animation* (pp. 131–140). Grenoble, France: Eurographics Association.

Chapter 6
Skeletal Animation with Anisotropic Materials

Abstract In this chapter, we present an integrated real-time system for animation of skeletal characters with anisotropic tissues. Existing geometrically-based skinning techniques suffer from obvious volume distortion artifact, and they cannot produce secondary dynamic motions, such as *jiggling* effects. *Physically-based skinning* with FEM models has high computational cost that restricts its practical applications. To solve these problems, we introduce a strain-based *Position Based Deformation* (PBD) framework for skeletal animation. It bridges the gap between geometric models and physically-based models, and achieves both efficient and physically-plausible performance. Natural secondary motion of soft tissues is produced. Anisotropic deformations are made possible with separately defined stretch and shear properties of the material, using the user-designed *frame-field*. Owing to the efficiency and stability of our proposed layered constraint solving scheme, we can achieve real-time performance, and the system is robust with large deformations and degenerate cases.

6.1 Introduction

In this work, we extend our research to more complicated deformable models with skeletons. Skeletal characters are widely used in animations, computer games, movies, etc. It is an active research field in computer graphics. There are still challenges in rigging and skinning techniques, with the goal to perform fast, stable and realistic character animation, as well as to achieve simple and intuitive control of material properties and dynamic behaviors.

Here, we develop a framework for animating skeletal characters, which combines traditional *skinning* and *dynamics simulation* of deformable objects:

- We present a fast skinning method with a physically based deformable model. The *position-based dynamics* framework is employed for its simplicity and stability, and a *strain-based constraint* is exploited instead of geometric constraints.

© Springer International Publishing Switzerland 2016
J. Cai et al., *Graphical Simulation of Deformable Models*,
DOI 10.1007/978-3-319-51031-6_6

- We have devised a new layered constraint solving scheme, which significantly increases the convergence rate of the constraint solver.
- Furthermore, we use an interactively generated *frame-field* in combination with strain-based constraint. It helps a user to intuitively control the anisotropic material properties along different directions. This controllability is a desirable feature in animation design.

Real-time animation with Physically-plausible deformations and secondary motions are obtained. Anisotropic deformations are produced, where stretch and shear properties of an anisotropic material can be defined separately. With good computational efficiency, stability and controllability, our approach is a promising method for practical applications.

Following a review of the related works in Sect. 6.2, we first introduce the new skeletal animation system in Sect. 6.3. A simple rigging scheme is introduced to bind a volumetric mesh with a skeleton. In Sect. 6.4, dynamic motion of the unconstrained nodes is simulated within a PBD framework, enhanced by strain-based constraints and a volume constraint. A layered constraint solving scheme is proposed for fast convergence. And thus, anisotropic material properties can be set with the help of a frame-field generated by the editing tool. In Sect. 6.5, real-time animations are demonstrated, with comparisons of performance with previous methods and analyses of results. Section Error! Reference source not found. concludes our techniques and discusses future work.

6.2   Related Work

In conventional skeletal animation, a character consists of a surface mesh (called *skin*) and a hierarchy of bones (called *skeleton*). A *rigged* mesh is controlled in accordance with the motion of the embedded skeleton. This is called *skinning*.

Linear blend skinning (LBS) [1] is a popular method for its simplicity and efficiency. The transformation matrix for each vertex of the rigged surface mesh is the weighted sum of those of its associated bones. However, in case of large rotating or bending motion, LBS suffers from the *candy-wrapper* and the *collapsing-joint* artifacts at some joint positions. *Dual-quaternion skinning* (DQS) [2, 3] resolves the problem, but it introduces the bulging-joint artifact when the bending angle is large. These skinning methods are purely geometrically-based and do not consider the underlying material properties of an animated character, which makes it difficult for them to generate both visually and physically-realistic results for versatile skeletal motions. Manual editing or post processing (e.g., [4]) is often needed for volume correction. A manual weight painting process for weight refinement is required, which is quite tricky and time consuming. Moreover, they cannot produce secondary dynamic motions and small deformation details, such as jiggling and bulging effects, which are critical to the physical realism of an animation. Handcrafting all these detailed deformations is not practical.

Physically based skinning methods, where deformations of a skeletal character are generated by dynamics simulation, have been developed in recent years. Based on continuum mechanics, it generates physically accurate skinning results with a high degree of realism, but at high computational cost. Capell et al. [5, 6] presented a framework of skeleton-driven character animation. It models a character with an elastic *control lattice* attached to its skeleton and uses a linear elastic model in the simulation, which is solved by the finite element method (FEM). Constructing the control lattice is laborious and time consuming, and its resolution is not high enough to avoid undesirable artifacts. Teran et al. [7] proposed a quasistatic FEM method for flesh simulation that can robustly deal with inverted elements, but the scheme ignores the inertial effect and thus cannot capture dynamic details of secondary motions. Gilles et al. [8] combined DQS with continuum mechanics, and formulated a generalized frame-based elastic model. The frame positions are updated in reaction to the internal forces instead of a scripted motion, thus the method cannot be applied to skeletal animation directly. A fast approach with nonlinear FEM proposed in [9] considers two-way interactions among the skeleton, the body, and the environment, and real-time or near real-time performance can be obtained with explicit time integration. However, it is well-known that explicit integration is only conditionally stable and not suitable for practical applications. Kim et al. [10] proposed a multi-domain subspace method to boost the simulation speed, but it requires a time-consuming pre-processing including domain decomposition, subspace basis analysis and cubature optimization, and the range of deformations is constrained within a subspace.

Position-based dynamics proposed by Müller et al. [11] provides a simple framework for dynamics simulation of deformable objects (refer to the survey paper [12]). The main advantages are its computational efficiency and stability. Explicit time integration can be used to produce stable results without suffering from overshooting problems. Thus it is suitable for real-time applications. Deul et al. [13] proposed a multi-layer surface model for character skinning within the PBD framework. It employs a method of shape matching with oriented particles [14] for elasticity simulation, and uses position-based constraints for contact handling, volume conservation and coupling of the skeleton with the deformable model. Rumman et al. [15, 16] presented a skeleton-driven deformable model with a volumetric mesh, which uses LBS and imposes three geometric constraints (stretch, volume, and bind constraints) within PBD. Geometric constraints which depend on the tessellation of the simulated mesh are used, thus making the deformation behaviors dependent on the mesh topology. Meanwhile, only isotropic deformations can be simulated by tuning the coefficients of the constraints.

In contrast, a strain-based constraint [Müller '14a], instead of geometric constraints, is exploited in our system. The constraint is defined in terms of a nonlinear *Green-Lagrange strain tensor* derived from solid mechanics [17]. Stiffness values of the constraints are independent of tessellation. Stretch and shear properties of a material are defined separately such that anisotropic deformations can be produced, with reference to the local frames generated by an interactive tool.

6.3   Formation of the Skeletal Animation System

6.3.1   Workflow of the System

The workflow of our framework of skeletal animation is shown in Fig. 6.1. The input data includes a tetrahedral (TET) mesh and a skeleton with motion capture (Mocap) data, as shown in Fig. 6.1a. The wireframe mesh represents the simulated TET mesh, and the pink-colored mesh is a high-resolution surface mesh embedded in the TET mesh for high-quality rendering (as in [18]). By applying a simple rigging method, the TET mesh is attached to the skeleton, as shown in Fig. 6.1b. Optionally, an interactive tool is used to define NURBS curves upon the TET mesh (Fig. 6.1c), which is used to generate a volumetric frame-field (Fig. 6.1d) that helps to set anisotropic material properties. A frame of the resulting real-time skeletal animation is shown in Fig. 6.1e. In this section, we explain the proposed rigging

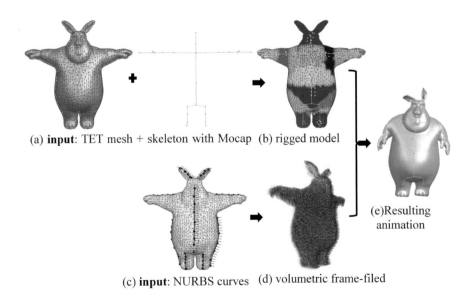

(a) **input**: TET mesh + skeleton with Mocap   (b) rigged model

(e)Resulting animation

(c) **input**: NURBS curves   (d) volumetric frame-filed

Fig. 6.1 Workflow of the skeletal animation framework

and skinning method, and how to generate a spatially varying frame-field for defining material properties.

6.3.2   A Simplified Rigging Scheme

A skeleton is represented as a hierarchical structure of bones and joints. In contrast with the LBS and DQS where many vertices are affected by multiple bones, a simple rigging scheme is proposed here: the tetrahedral elements intersected by the skeleton are constrained, and each constrained element is only attached to one bone, which makes the advanced weighting functions as in the LBS or DQS unnecessary. Therefore, it relieves an animator from a painful weight painting procedure.

Each frame of the skeletal motion data consists of the local translational and rotational transformations of each joint. The global transformation of each bone is computed as an accumulated transformation from the root joint to the current joint, which is represented by a 4×4 homogeneous matrix. In contrast to the LBS where each vertex of the rigged mesh is transformed by a weighted sum of the global transformations of its associated bones, a simple skinning scheme is sufficient here: the current position v' of a constrained node in an animation-frame is computed as

$$v' = MT^{-1}v_0 \qquad (6.1)$$

where v_0 is the global position of the node in the initial configuration (i.e., the rest pose), M is the current global transformation matrix of its attached bone, and T is a transformation matrix defining the global position of the bone in the rest pose, which is only a translation matrix. This simple skinning scheme binds a TET mesh with an associated skeleton.

6.4   Dynamics Simulation Within the PBD Framework

By considering the TET mesh as an elastic deformable object, the unconstrained nodes are then updated by a dynamics simulation driven by the skeletal motion. Instead of formulating the simulation as a rigorous solid mechanics problem and solving it by the commonly used finite element method [19] at a high computational cost, the PBD framework is employed here for its fast and stable performance.

Algorithm 1. Skeleton-driven PBD simulation

---

(1)   Initialize positions and velocities: x_0, and v_0;

(2)   **while** (simulating)

  // update skeleton constraint at a Mocap frame   .

(3)   update a motion frame (frameID++);

(4)   update constrained nodes;

  // symplectic Euler integration

(5) $v_{t+1} \leftarrow v_t + h * m_i^{-1} * f_{ext}$;

(6) $x_{t+1} \leftarrow x_t + h * v_{t+1}$;

  //solve the constraints by projection

(7)   **for** (i=0; i<#iterations; i++)

(8) $x'_{t+1} \leftarrow \text{ConstraintSolver}(x_{t+1})$;

(9)   **end**

  // update velocities

(10) $v_{t+1} \leftarrow (x'_{t+1} - x_t)/h$;

(11)   DampedVelocity(v_{t+1});

(12) **end**

Combined with the motion data, the simulation loop of the PBD is depicted in Algorithm 1. In the first step, a motion frame is updated and the positions of the constrained nodes are updated by the simple skinning in Eq. (6.1). Then, a *symplectic Euler integration* computes the predicted positions (as in steps 5 and 6). Here h denotes the time-step size, f_{ext} the external force with only gravity considered here. m_i^{-1} is the inverse mass of each node, which is set to zero for a constrained node. The key component of the algorithm is the constraint solver (in steps 7–9). It corrects the blindly predicted positions in the time integration step by iteratively solving different constraints in a Gauss-Seidel-like way, which is called *positional projection*. Finally, the nodal velocities are updated and damped in steps 10 and 11.

6.4.1 Strain-Based Constraint

Instead of geometric constraints used in the previous works for skeletal animation [13, 15, 20], a strain-based constraint [Müller '14a] is exploited here, which adds more physical authenticity to the PBD method. Furthermore, anisotropic dynamic behaviors can be obtained.

In solid mechanics, deformation can be measured by a strain tensor defined as $C = \frac{1}{2}(F^{T}F - I) \in \mathbb{R}^{3 \times 3}$, called the *Green-Lagrange strain tensor*, where $F \in \mathbb{R}^{3 \times 3}$ is the *deformation gradient*, $I \in \mathbb{R}^{3 \times 3}$ is the identity matrix. Given a TET element with its nodal positions (X_0, X_1, X_2, X_3) in the initial configuration and (x_0, x_1, x_2, x_3) in the deformed configuration, the deformation gradient can be approximately computed as

$$F = D_s D_m^{-1}, \tag{6.2}$$

where $D_s = [x_1 - x_0, x_2 - x_0, x_3 - x_0]$, and $D_m^{-1} = [X_1 - X_0, X_2 - X_0, X_3 - X_0]^{-1}$. Here, D_m^{-1} can be pre-computed, and F is constant within an element. The nonlinear strain tensor is rotation-invariant, thus it supports large deformations.

A constraint function can be defined based on the strain tensor, as

$$C(x_0, x_1, x_2, x_3) = \frac{1}{2}\left(F^{T}F - I\right) = \mathbf{0}. \tag{6.3}$$

With this constraint satisfied, a deformed element can be restored to its initial pose. Since C is symmetric, six scalar functions of constraints are obtained here, including three stretch constraints with respect to the diagonal components and three shear constraints with respect to the off-diagonal components, written as $C_{ij}(x_0, x_1, x_2, x_3) = 0, i < j$. For faster convergence of the constraint solver, we used a linearized stretch constraint [21] as $C_{ii}(x_0, x_1, x_2, x_3) = \sqrt{S_{ii}} - 1 = 0$, where S_{ii} are the diagonal elements of $F^{T}F$.

In contrast with geometric constraints on edge lengths and element volumes, the strain-based constraint is independent of the mesh tessellation, and provides the user with more control over the material properties along different directions. Later we design an interactive tool to define a frame-field as a reference for defining the anisotropic material properties.

6.4.2 Volume Constraint

Theoretically, a deformed element can be restored to its original shape if the strain-based constraints are completely satisfied. However, since the strain-based constraint is solved in a Gauss-Seidel-like manner and only by a few iterations, an additional volume constraint for volume conservation is useful and necessary to deal with scenarios of large deformations. From the fact that $J = \det(F)$ represents the fraction of volume change of an element, where $J = 1$ means no volume change, a volume constraint can be derived as

$$J(\pmb{x}_0, \pmb{x}_1, \pmb{x}_2, \pmb{x}_3) - 1 = 0. \tag{6.4}$$

The advantage of this volume constraint is that inverted or degenerated elements can be restored without special treatments such as the methods in [22, 23].

6.4.3 The Layered Constraint Solver

A fundamental scheme for solving a constraint function can be formulated as follows [11]. Given a constraint function $c(\pmb{x}) = 0$ where $\pmb{x}$ is a vector of constrained variables (e.g., $\pmb{x} = (\pmb{x}_0, \pmb{x}_1, \pmb{x}_2, \pmb{x}_3)$ for a TET element), the positional correction $\Delta \pmb{x}$ can be obtained by firstly applying a first-order Taylor expansion as

$$c(\pmb{x} + \Delta \pmb{x}) \approx c(\pmb{x}) + \nabla_{\pmb{x}} c \cdot \Delta \pmb{x} = 0, \tag{6.5}$$

where $\nabla_{\pmb{x}} c = \frac{\partial c}{\partial \pmb{x}}$ is the gradient of c with respect to $\pmb{x}$. Then by restricting the direction of $\Delta \pmb{x}$ as $\Delta \pmb{x} = \lambda \nabla_{\pmb{x}} c$ for the conservation of the linear and angular momentum, we have

$$\Delta \pmb{x} = k \left(-\frac{c(\pmb{x})}{|\nabla_{\pmb{x}} c|^2} \right) \nabla_{\pmb{x}} c, \tag{6.6}$$

where k is the stiffness defining the strength of the constraint. By considering the nodal weight $w_i = m_i^{-1}$, the nodal correction vector is finally computed as

$$\Delta \pmb{x}_i = w_i k \left(-\frac{c(\pmb{x})}{\sum_{j=0}^{3} w_j |\nabla_{\pmb{x}_j} c|^2} \right) \nabla_{\pmb{x}_i} c, \tag{6.7}$$

The strength of a certain constraint can be defined by a corresponding stiffness k, thus the final position correction is taken as $k\Delta \pmb{x}$. This projection process is usually done by a predefined number of iterations in a Gauss-Seidel manner, i.e., it solves the constraint element-wisely, and the resulting positional correction of each element immediately affects following updates. The constraint solver actually propagates the deformations from place to place across the whole TET mesh. It converges to an equilibrium state if an infinite number of iterations are taken.

There are limitations with the constraint solving scheme. First, it converges slowly, meaning that it requires many iterations to converge, especially for high resolution TET meshes (i.e., it takes longer time to propagate a deformation across a mesh with a higher resolution). This also means that the mechanical behaviors

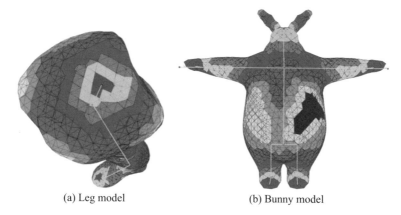

(a) Leg model   (b) Bunny model

Fig. 6.2 TET elements are re-ordered in different layers, so that the constraints can be solved layer-wisely (layer rendered in different colors)

depend on mesh resolution. Second, the order of constraints also affects convergence, meaning that if the constraints of elements are solved in a different order, it will produce different deformation behaviors (i.e., show different material stiffness).

In our animation system, the constrained nodes moves with the skeleton and the rest free nodes are updated by the constraint solver. Based on the fact that deformations are propagated from the constrained nodes to the free nodes, we reorder the elements into layers according to the distances from the skeleton, such that each bone is surrounded by multi-layers of elements, as illustrated in Fig. 6.2 for two TET meshes (a *leg* model and a *bunny* model). Then, the solver solves the constraints upon elements layer-by-layer.

In order to further improve the iteration convergence rate, during the first few iterations, we artificially increases the nodal masses of this layer to consolidate the previous updates after updating nodal positions of each layer (named *consolidating iterations* here), and reset the masses to the original configuration for later iterations. This *layered constraint solver* requires much less iterations for each animation frame than the unordered scheme used in previous works. Moreover, it relieves the dependency on different mesh resolutions by increasing the number of consolidating iterations for a higher resolution mesh. More implementation details and results are discussed later.

6.4.4   Frame-Field Augmented Anisotropic Model

Soft tissues of a character often exhibit anisotropic elastic behaviors, thus it is necessary to define a spatially varying frame-field to help specify material properties in local frames, as shown in Fig. 6.1d. Here we use the interactive tool devised in the previous chapter (refer to Sect. 5.4) to generate the frame-field.

In order to augment the simulation with the frame-field control, the deformation gradient [as in Eq. (6.2)] of each element should be computed in the local frames as

$$F' = \left(Q_i^T D_s\right)\left(Q_i^T D_m\right)^{-1}, \tag{6.8}$$

where Q_i is the local frame matrix in Eq. (5.4). The inverse matrix of the second term can be pre-computed.

Therefore, the constraint solver yields a local correction vector $\Delta x_i'$, which needs to be transformed back to a global correction vector $\Delta x_i = Q_i \Delta x_i'$.

6.4.5 Discussion

A decoupled shear constraint $C_{ij}(x_0, x_1, x_2, x_3) = \dfrac{\sqrt{S_{ij}}}{|S_{ij}|} = 0, i < j$ was also proposed in [21], which decouples shear from stretch and penalizes only the angular deformation. However, this decoupled shear constraint is nonlinear along the projection direction. It causes overshooting problems, leading to simulation failure (which happens in our experiments) when large bending angles occur at the joints. Thus, non-decoupled shear constraint, which affects the stretch of an element, is applied here. Combining it with the volume constraint might result in an over-constrained system, producing jittering artifacts. This issue can be solved by decreasing the stiffness of the volume constraint.

Another issue with the PBD framework is that material stiffness depends on not only the constraint coefficients, but also the time-step size and the number of iterations in the constraint solver. Here we set the time step to be consistent with the frame-rate of the skeleton motion, and set a constant number of iterations.

6.5 Computational Results

In the skeletal animation system, a high resolution surface mesh is embedded in a coarse tetrahedral mesh for the final rendering, and is deformed by barycentric interpolation of the simulated mesh. A coarse volumetric mesh is useful to boost performance speed. Kinematic motion capture (Mocap) data is obtained from the open Mocap databases [24, 25, 26] in *BVH* format (refer to [27] for specification). And we use Blender software [28] to edit the skeletal structure in order to match it to a character model. We implemented the system in C++, and all the algorithms are CPU-based.

6.5.1 Setting of Constrained Elements

Initially, we constrained all the skeleton-intersected elements (as shown in Fig. 6.3a, constrained nodes are rendered as yellow points), which turned out to produce undesirable artifacts with the skinning results. If the nodes of a constrained element are attached to different bones, outliers are produced due to the volume constraint. Rumman et al. [15, 16] solved this problem by adding an additional bind constraint, which maintains the distance between a node and a related bone; however, it adds more computational cost.

Here, we establish a simple rule that tetrahedra intersected by more than one bone (i.e., around the joints) should not be constrained, i.e., there is only a one-to-one relationship between constrained elements and attached bones. Figure 6.3d shows the corrected constrained nodes, and Fig. 6.3e, f show correct deformation behaviors around all the joints. This strategy makes the *bind constraint* unnecessary, which saves computational cost.

6.5.2 Comparison with Conventional Skinning Methods

Here we compare our method with the popular LBS and DQS in different scenarios. As shown in Fig. 6.4a, the LBS method suffers from a well-known candy-wrapper artifact when performing a twisting motion. In Fig. 6.5b, the DQS suffers from a bugling-joint artifact with a bending motion, whereas the LBS produces a better deformation (Fig. 6.5a); a textured-cylinder model is used here to provide a better visual reference for comparison. Therefore, none of these methods can produce satisfactory deformations in all scenarios. Since our skinning method works with physically-based constraints, realistic deformations can be produced without suffering from these artifacts. The volume is well preserved, as shown in Figs. 6.4b and 6.5c. Furthermore, there is no need of a weight-painting refinement process as is used in the previous methods.

6.5.3 Comparison with Unordered Constraint Solver

Here we compare the results of unordered constraint solver and our layered constraint solver. As shown Fig. 6.6, a jumping leg model (with 24387 TET elements) is simulated, with all the three rows are simulated by the same constraint coefficients and time-step size. The unordered solver converges slowly, as shown in Fig. 6.6a, that after 10 iterations it is far from convergence, it needs 50 iterations to obtain satisfactory behaviors as shown Fig. 6.6b. In contrast, the reordered solver as

(a)   **(b)**   **(c)**

(d)   **(e)**   **(f)**

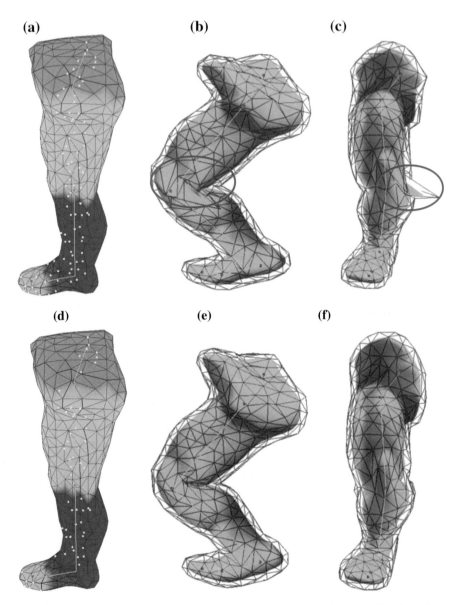

Fig. 6.3 Constrained elements by the skeleton. In (**a**), all the elements intersected by the skeleton are constrained, producing outliers shown in (**b**), (**c**). In (**d**), bone-shared elements are excluded, and correct deformations are produced shown in (**e**) and (**f**)

shown Fig. 6.6c takes only 10 iterations (with the first 6 as consolidating iterations) to achieve similar results. This validates the fast convergence rate of the proposed ordered solving scheme, which greatly reduces computational cost for solving the constraints.

Fig. 6.4 Comparison with the LBS method: **a** LBS skinning with a candy-wrapper artifact; **b** Skinning by our method

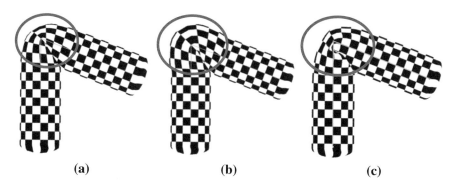

Fig. 6.5 Comparison with the LBS and DQS. **a** LBS skinning; **b** DQS skinning with a bulging-joint artifact; **c** Skinning by our method

For the unordered solver, there is a large difference of convergence rates among meshes with different resolutions. In Fig. 6.7, a lower-resolution leg model (with 3452 TET elements) is simulated with the same constraint coefficients and time-step size as in Fig. 6.6. As shown in Fig. 6.7a, the unordered solver with 10 iterations converges much faster with the lower-resolution mesh than the high-resolution one in Fig. 6.6a. This poses difficulty for deformation control of meshes with different resolutions, due to large performance differences among them. The ordered solver larges alleviates this problem. As shown in Fig. 6.7b, with the same setting with Fig. 6.6c, the results show stiffer material properties than the former one; it can be adjusted by decreasing the number of consolidating iterations (2 consolidating iterations as in Fig. 6.7c) to achieve similar deformation behaviors with Fig. 6.6c. Therefore, deformation control can be done at similar performance level by using the ordered solver.

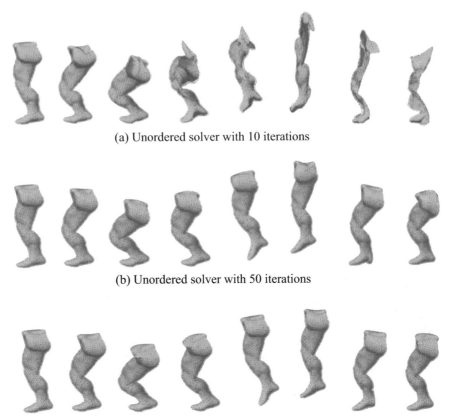

(a) Unordered solver with 10 iterations

(b) Unordered solver with 50 iterations

(c) Layered constraint solver with 10 iterations (contains 6 consolidating iterations)

Fig. 6.6 Comparison between unordered solver and our layered constraint solver

6.5.4 Comparison of Isotropic and Anisotropic Deformations

Here, we demonstrate the simulation of a frame-field augmented simulation of a fat bunny model (obtained from Blender open movie project [29]). Figure 6.8a shows a skeleton-constrained TET mesh; Fig. 6.8b shows the NURBS curves and associated RMFs for generation of the frame-field in Fig. 6.8c.

In Fig. 6.9, we show the deformations of models with isotropic and anisotropic materials. Without a reference frame-field, we can only define isotropic materials: the strain-based constraints are solved in a single global frame, and there are only two strain-based coefficients (i.e., one stretch stiffness and one shear stiffness). Isotropic deformations are shown in Fig. 6.9a. With the help of the frame-field, where each frame is represented by three axes (r, g, b) rendered in red, green and

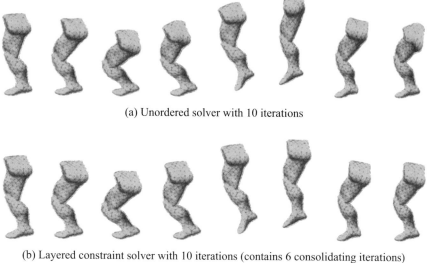

(a) Unordered solver with 10 iterations

(b) Layered constraint solver with 10 iterations (contains 6 consolidating iterations)

(b) Layered constraint solver with 10 iterations (contains 2 consolidating iterations)

Fig. 6.7 Comparison the results of unordered solver and our layered constraint solver, for a low-resolution mesh

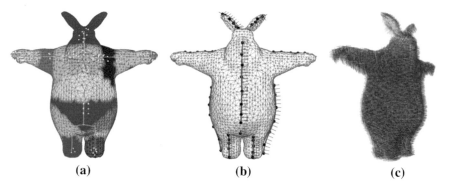

(a)   **(b)**   **(c)**

Fig. 6.8 a Skeletal constraint; **b** NURBS curves and associated RMFs; **c** The generated frame-field

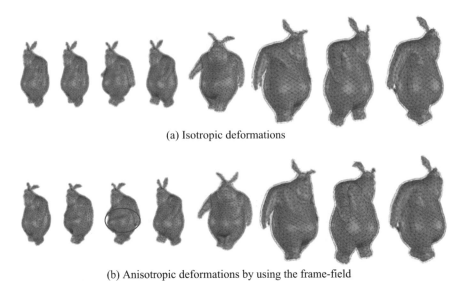

(a) Isotropic deformations

(b) Anisotropic deformations by using the frame-field

Fig. 6.9 Comparison between isotropic and anisotropic deformations

blue colors, respectively. In total, six constraint coefficients can be defined: three stretch coefficients and three shear coefficients along three directions of each local frame for each TET element. Here we adjust the six parameters to define an anisotropic material. The anisotropic setting exhibits more complicated and expressive deformations than the isotropic one, such as the wrinkles formed at its belly and more flexible behaviors at the ears, as shown in Fig. 6.9b. Using geometrical constraints as in previous works (as in [15, 16]), it is difficult to define anisotropic materials, especially for a TET mesh with an irregular mesh grid.

6.5.5 Comparison with Previous Skeletal Animation Using PBD

In related work of skeletal animation by Rumman et al. [15, 16], a straightforward *two-pass* deformation scheme was proposed: first, the LBS scheme is applied on a whole TET mesh; second, all the vertex positions are corrected by a PBD simulation with respect to three geometrical constraints (stretch, volume and bind constraints).

Compared with their work: (1) our method avoids the LBS computation, and no weight function needs to be defined; instead, only a simple and fast rigging is required to update the constrained nodes; (2) Strain-based constraints instead of geometrical constraints are exploited, which makes the definition of material properties independent of mesh grid, and anisotropic materials can be defined; no bind constraint is needed to maintain the rest distance between a node and its projection on the skeleton. (3) With the layered constraint solving scheme, our solver converges much faster, which means better computational efficiency.

6.5.6 Performance Analysis

More simulation results are shown in Figs. 6.10 and 6.11, which demonstrate the effectiveness and robustness of our method against large ranges of motions.

An un-optimized implementation of the system is done with CPU-based algorithms in C++. All the examples are executed on a desktop with Intel Core CPUs (i7-4770 @3.40 GHz). The time-step size of the constraint solver is set to be consistent with the frame-rate of the Mocap data (120 Hz with the male model, and others with 30 Hz or 25 Hz). Statistics and simulation performance of the examples are shown in Table 6.1. Simulation performance with different models. It shows that the frame-field augmented simulation only costs a small fraction of time more than the one without a frame-field, which involves local-frame computations. All the simulations are done within 10 iterations of the constraint solver, thanks to the layered solving scheme. Therefore, real-time performance can be achieved.

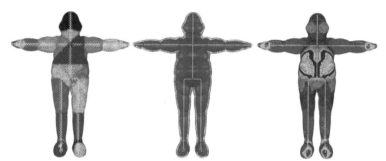

(a) (*from left to right*): a rigged model; a surface mesh embedded in a TET mesh;
multiple layers of elements in different colors

(b) Some animation frames

Fig. 6.10 Some animation frames (the surface model is courtesy of Kim [9])

(a) (*from left to right*): a rigged model; a surface mesh embedded in a TET mesh; multiple layers of elements

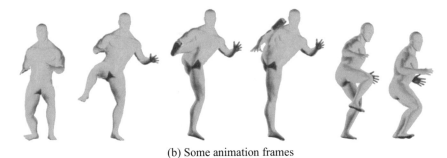

(b) Some animation frames

Fig. 6.11 Skeletal animation of a male model

Table 6.1 Simulation performance with different models

Model	#Total elements	#Unconstrained elements	Time-step size (s)	Number of Iterations (total/consolidating)	Simulation Time (ms)	
					Without frame-field	With frame-field
Cylinder	2214	2169	0.042	3/1	2.3	2.8
Leg (low resolution)	3452	3373	0.033	10/2	11.6	14.6
				10/6	11.8	14.6
Arm	10760	10433	0.042	6/2	21.5	27.1
Leg (high resolution)	24837	24,670	0.033	10/6	87.5	108.5
Bunny	27350	27,136	0.033	4/1	37.8	48.3
Male	74288	73,647	0.008	10/1	258.5	335.1
Fatman	89876	89,306	0.033	10/2	317.7	408.5

6.6 Summary

We have presented a real-time system that exploits the advantages of both dynamics simulation of deformable objects and skeletal animation. A strain-based PBD framework is used in the geometrically based skinning techniques such as LBS and

DQS. This turns out to be effective and efficient for animating characters consisting of soft tissues. Natural secondary motion of soft tissues can be produced, while anisotropic deformation behaviors can be intuitively controlled by using a user-designed frame-field. Stretch and shear coefficients can be easily tuned to change material stiffness along different directions. The constraint solver converges quickly with an ordered layered solving scheme. Stable and real-time performance can be achieved, thanks to the PBD framework.

There are still rooms for improvement in the future. First, volume can be well preserved for each element; however, without dealing with self-contact, self-penetration artifacts can occur. In the future, self-collision constraint will be exploited in order to obtain more accurate deformation behaviors. Second, currently there is only a one-way interaction between the skeleton and the simulated mesh, that is, motion of the mesh is driven by the skeleton. Furthermore, a two-way coupling approach can be incorporated into the system. The motion of the soft tissues can also affect the movements of the pre-defined motion of skeleton. This would be helpful to apply a same Mocap data to characters of different sizes and weights, and re-generate different locomotion that respects their different characteristics. Third, better tetrahedralization algorithm can also be developed to generate TET mesh with qualified layers of elements, which would improve the performance of the layered constraint solver.

References

1. Magnenat-Thalmann, N., Laperrire, R., & Thalmann, D. (1988). Joint-dependent local deformations for hand animation and object grasping. In *Proceedings on Graphics Interface '88*, Citeseer.
2. Kavan, L., et al. (2007). Skinning with dual quaternions. In *Proceedings of the 2007 Symposium on Interactive 3D Graphics and Games*. ACM.
3. Kavan, L., et al. (2008). Geometric skinning with approximate dual quaternion blending. *ACM Transactions on Graphics (TOG), 27*(4), 105.
4. Kim, Y., & Han, J. (2014). Bulging-free dual quaternion skinning. *Computer Animation and Virtual Worlds, 25*(3–4), 321–329.
5. Capell, S., et al. (2002). Interactive skeleton-driven dynamic deformations. *ACM Transactions on Graphics, 21*(3), 586–593.
6. Capell, S., et al. (2007). Physically based rigging for deformable characters. *Graphical Models, 69*(1), 71–87.
7. Teran, J., et al. (2005). Robust quasistatic finite elements and flesh simulation. In *Proceedings of the 2005 ACM SIGGRAPH/Eurographics symposium on Computer animation* (pp. 181–190). Los Angeles, California: ACM.
8. Gilles, B., et al. (2011). Frame-based elastic models. *ACM Transactions on Graphics, 30*(2), 1–12.
9. Kim, J., & Pollard, N. S. (2011). Fast simulation of skeleton-driven deformable body characters. *ACM Transactions on Graphics, 30*(5), 1–19.
10. Kim, T., & James, D.L. (2011). Physics-based character skinning using multi-domain subspace deformations. In *Proceedings of the 2011 ACM SIGGRAPH/Eurographics Symposium on Computer Animation* (pp. 63–72). Vancouver, British Columbia, Canada: ACM.

11. Müller, M., et al. (2007). Position based dynamics. *Journal of Visual Communication and Image Representation, 18*(2), 109–118.

12. Bender, J., et al. (2014). Position-based simulation of continuous materials. *Computers and Graphics, 44*, 1–10.

13. Deul, C., & Bender, J. (2013). Physically-based character skinning. *VRIPHYS, 13*, 25–34.

14. Müller, M., & Chentanez, N. (2011). Solid simulation with oriented particles. *ACM Transactions on Graphics (TOG), 30*(4), 92.

15. Rumman, N. A., & M. Fratarcangeli. (2014). Position based skinning of skeleton-driven deformable characters. In *Proceedings of the 30th Spring Conference on Computer Graphics*. ACM.

16. Rumman, N. A. & Fratarcangeli, M. (2015). Position-based skinning for soft articulated characters. In *Computer Graphics Forum*. Wiley Online Library.

17. Bower, A. F. (2009). Applied mechanics of solids. CRC press.

18. Müller, M., & Gross, M. (2004). Interactive virtual materials. In *Proceedings of Graphics Interface* (pp. 239–246). London, Ontario, Canada: Canadian Human-Computer Communications Society.

19. Sifakis, E., & Barbic, J. (2012). FEM simulation of 3D deformable solids: a practitioner's guide to theory, discretization and model reduction. In *ACM SIGGRAPH 2012 Courses*. ACM.

20. Abu Rumman, N., & Fratarcangeli, M. (2015). Position-based skinning for soft articulated characters. *Computer Graphics Forum, 34*(6), 240–250.

21. Müller, M., et al. (2014). Strain based dynamics. In *Proceedings of ACM SIGGRAPH/ EUROGRAPHICS Symposium on Computer Animation (SCA)*. Copenhagen.

22. Irving, G., Teran, J., & Fedkiw, R. (2006). Tetrahedral and hexahedral invertible finite elements. *Graphical Models, 68*(2), 66–89.

23. Stomakhin, A., et al. (2012). Energetically Consistent Invertible Elasticity. In *Eurographics/ ACM SIGGRAPH Symposium on Computer Animation*. The Eurographics Association.

24. Huang, J., et al. (2006). Geometrically based potential energy for simulating deformable objects. *The Visual Computer, 22*(9–11), 740–748.

25. CMU, *CMU Graphics Lab Motion Capture Database*. http://mocap.cs.cmu.edu/

26. NUS, *NUS Mocap Database*, in *National University of Singapore*. http://animation.comp.nus. edu.sg/nusmocap.html. Created with funding from NUS AcRF R-252-000-429-133.

27. Biovision, *BVH File Specifications page*. http://www.character-studio.net/bvh_file_specification. htm

28. Blender, *Blender, free and open source 3D creation suite*. https://www.blender.org

29. Foundation, B. (2008). *Big Buck Bunny*. https://peach.blender.org/

Chapter 7
Discussions and Conclusions

Abstract In this chapter, we conclude this monograph with the major techniques developed, and give our perspectives on the future directions of research in this field. This book presents our research on dynamics simulation of deformable models applied in computer graphics field. Both geometrically-based and physically-based approaches have been studied in our work. We focus on deformable objects of anisotropic materials, which are less exploited than those of isotropic materials in existing work. Deformable objects of anisotropic materials are commonly seen in the real world, which exhibit more complicated and flexible mechanical behaviors. Therefore, compared with isotropic models, anisotropic models bring new challenges for designing stable and efficient simulation approaches, and for developing deformation control methods.

7.1 Reviews and Remarks

Our main goals are: (1) developing stable and efficient approaches for dynamics simulation of anisotropic models, which can be applied in interactive or real-time applications; (2) developing control methods to achieve directable deformation behaviors of anisotropic models. Our major contributions are as follows:

- Firstly, we have studied transversely isotropic materials for simulation of deformable objects with fibrous structures. A novel fiber-field incorporated CLFEM model is developed, which is computationally efficient and allows large deformations. Transversely isotropic deformations can be intuitively controlled by a user input fiber-field.
- Secondly, we have further investigated deformable objects of orthotropic materials, which have more complicated material properties and more flexible mechanical behaviors. A novel interactive tool is designed to produce a smooth frame-field inside a volumetric mesh, and a quaternion Laplacian smoothing algorithm is developed in order to generate such a frame-field. We have formulated a CLFEM model augmented with an orthotropic frame-field. Robust

dynamics simulation is achieved by a stable tuning of material properties and dealing with inverted and degenerate deformations.

- Thirdly, we have developed a novel method of physically-based skeletal character animation. Deformations of a deformable character are driven by the motion of an embedded skeleton, combining conventional skeletal animation with dynamics simulation. To further improve the efficiency and stability of simulation, we exploit the PBD framework instead of the rigorous FEM model. A strain-based constrain is employed instead of geometric constraint used in previous works. A new layered constraint solving scheme is devised for fast convergence. This bridges the gap between PBD and rigorous physical approaches. The frame-field used in the FEM model can also be incorporated in the strain-based constraint; anisotropic deformation behaviors can be controlled intuitively and stably by setting different constraint coefficients with respect to the local frames of the frame-field.

The proposed approaches can be easily applied in many graphics applications, such as soft tissues simulation in virtual surgery, computer games and animations.

7.2 Perspectives

In computer graphics research, a goal is to simulate real-world phenomena. Dynamics simulation of deformable objects is still an active research area, with the goal of pursuing more stable, efficient and physically-realistic results. There are some issues that are not investigated in our current work, but they are also of great importance to a practical simulation framework. We might further investigate the following issues in the future:

- To improve the simulation performance of our current implementation, parallel computing algorithms need to be designed, either by using multi-threading on CPUs, or by harnessing the computing power of modern GPUs.
- Collision detection and response are still two challenging problems for deformable objects simulation. They are important for simulating phenomenon of self-interaction and interactions with environments.
- Since real-world deformable objects are not ideally elastic models, mechanical behaviors such as elastoplastic deformations and fractures also need to be considered for improved realism.
- In a simulation system, besides deformable objects (with different dimensions such as 1D ropes, 2D shells and 3D solids), there are often other object types such as rigid bodies, gases, and liquids. A unified physics framework has become popular in visual effects in recent years (e.g., a unified PBD framework

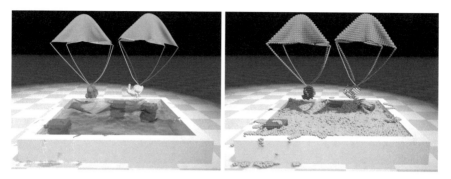

Fig. 7.1 Unified particle physics for real-time applications [1]

is shown in Fig. 7.1 [1]). With a unified dynamics solver, different types of objects that were previously simulated with different solvers can interact with each other in a fully-coupled way. However, there are still challenges for object representations, efficient solvers, modeling methods with physics support, etc.

Reference

1. Macklin, M., et al. (2014). Unified particle physics for real-time applications. *ACM Transactions on Graphics (TOG), 33*(4), 153.

Printed in the United States
By Bookmasters